Santrean,

M000309405

Spiritual Seduction

Secrets, Sin, Stress, Struggle, Yet Surviving

Enjoy your Reading

God's Blessings

Spiritual Seduction

Secrets, Sin, Stress, Struggle, Yet Surviving

Dr. Gloria M. Milow

Publishing

I was seventeen years old and became my pastor's mistress and a madam for his fellow ministers in the gospel. Even while riding down Century Boulevard in Los Angeles today, there are numerous hotels that I recall frequenting, yet my purpose was not solely for lodging. One escapade led to another, and I later realized I was not trusting in God but rather putting my trust in man. Simply put, I got caught up in a lifestyle that I now know I should have never endured. Thank God for His mighty power because He is the only one who enables us to transition from where we find ourselves to where He wants us to be.

There may be a number of sexual references and strong language in the book. This book is not designed to offend but rather to paint the true picture of what transpired.

Names have been changed to protect the privacy of the true identities of those involved

Published by:
MG's Books
3645 Marketplace Blvd
Suite 130-110
East Point, Georgia 30344
www.mgsbooks.com
www.mgsministries.com
(678) 491-5644

In conjunction with:
Old Mountain Press, Inc.
2542 S. Edgewater Dr.
Fayetteville, NC 28303
www.OldMountainPress.com

Copyright © 2008 Spiritual Seduction
Interior text design by Tom Davis
Cover Layout by Simone Adams
Edited by Alonia Jernigan and Phamesha LaSha Johnson
ISBN: 978-0-9793537-0-3
Library of Congress Control Number: 2008910041

First Edition
Printed and bound in the United States of America by Morris Publishing • www.morrispublishing.com • 800-650-7888
1 2 3 4 5 6 7 8 9 10

Contents

Prologue

Doing over 85 miles on I-405 in my black on black BMW, I couldn't wait to see Teddy. I knew that whenever I spent time with him there were always gifts, dope and lots of money to follow. I arrived at The Westin about 45 minutes later than I was expected. I knew that with Teddy, routine was out the door. He loved the excitement of something new each time so I purposely stayed at the dinner table a little longer with Reverend Hudson and Momma after Sunday's dinner.

Everyone always came over to our house on Sunday afternoons to recap after each sermon and do some light gossiping about the newcomers, misfits and backsliders at church. Momma was known to cook the best home-cooked meals and have the latest scandals on the local church folk. On this particular Sunday, she made golden fried catfish, baked macaroni and cheese, smothered pork chops, tender oxtails, savory mustard and collard greens, smothered creamed corn, fluffy mashed potatoes, fresh green peas from our garden, moist red velvet cake, sweet banana pudding, pound cake from scratch, and homemade buttermilk biscuits. I just about ate everything. I left my two children, Marilyn, and Jaray, Jr. with Momma. I wanted to be sure to put on an extraordinary performance for Teddy tonight.

After showering, putting on oil, fragrances and jewels I made sure to put on a red ruffled bra over my round perky breasts, matching lace panties, red thigh highs and red 6-inch pumps. And because I told Momma I was on my way to afternoon services I threw on a floral floor length dress.

When I arrived at The Westin I was overcome with fear and anxiety. So I valet parked and popped the trunk, got out the car and went for my purple liquor flask for a swig of my grandmother's famous peach brandy. After drinking the contents, I had the courage needed to face what lied ahead of me in Room 2214.

I walked in the lobby, went toward the elevator doors and pressed the arrow pointing up. Once inside I pushed the 22 button and the doors closed. As I rode the elevator up my nerves had settled and I started to feel the confidence and self-assurance I needed to face Teddy. When I got to the door I knocked lightly waiting for a response. To my surprise, there was no answer. I knocked again with the same intensity, but again no answer. I thought that maybe he was in the bathroom or he could have fallen asleep because I took so long to come over. So the next time, I knocked hard enough for him to hear me if he was in the bathroom and loud enough to wake him up but again, no answer.

"Shit," I thought to myself. "I can't go home. Momma thinks that I'm at church and she's got the kids. Where can I go? Where can I go?"

As I turned to walk away and was half way down the hall, I heard a familiar voice ask, "Why are you so late?" As I turned around, I saw Teddy. He looked agitated but he was weak for me so I knew that my charm would wear him down.

"Daddy, I wanted to get something real special for you. I'm late because I had to go to the mall to pick it up," I said as I started walking toward him.

"Oh yeah, what you got for me?" Teddy said.

"I don't know if I should show you. You look like you're annoyed with me for being late." I pouted. "All I wanted to do was make you feel good tonight." I stroked his chest and moved in closer and looked him in his eyes. "Maybe I should just go back home." As I turned to walk away he grabbed my arm and pulled me in the room.

"Hey baby, I'm sorry," he said. "I'm just a little tired. I worked especially hard today. Maybe we can make each other feel better."

Check Mate.

I went in the bathroom to freshen up. I took off my floral dress.

I checked for a stench and I sprayed myself with perfume.

Body odor, absent.

I checked my makeup.

Flawless.

And I did the breath check.

Fresh.

When I walked into the room, Teddy was sitting at the table drinking his favorite cocktail, Gin and tonic, while sniffing some lines of coke. When he looked up and saw me he was immobilized. I stood like a gazelle in my red patent leather stilettos. By this time I was no longer scrawny like in my elementary school days. My skin was flawless, the color of clover honey. My legs and thighs were soft, long, thick and beautiful. My hips stretched from east to west and my ass was now firm, round, and fat. I was envied by all because my waist was petite and my abs were tight. My titties were big; I now wore a 36 C bra. They were the size of melons round, perky, and succulent. I was without a doubt my daddy's child because my neck was elongated, my eyes were round and light brown and my hair was dark brown, long and curly with natural brown streaks.

I looked down on the TV stand and Teddy had my favorite party favors waiting for me: about 10 perfectly rolled up joints, a lighter, and a glass of Gin and 7-Up. I put the joint to my mouth and lit it. I took a long hard drag. Teddy continued to stare at me as his manhood appeared to rise in his white Fruit of the Looms boxers. As I stood there and the euphoric state started to take over, I leisurely walked toward the hotel room's stereo and looked for a radio station playing a song that I could seductively dance to. It was just my luck, Al Green's "I'm Still in Love with You" was going off and The Isley Brothers "In Between the Sheets" started to play. With glass and joint still in hand, I began to dance slow and seductively to the voice and sounds of Ron Isley.

I wanted to put on a show for Teddy that he would never forget. I looked over on the nightstand and grabbed the Johnson's baby oil and poured it all over my body and lingerie. As I stood in the middle of the king sized bed, I rotated and popped my hips to every beat of the song. I caressed and rubbed my body parts as if I was alone in my bedroom. I sucked my erect nipples and spanked my ass to every "Ooh" and "Ahh" of the song. My body gyrated and jerked so hard that I was excited by my own performance. My pussy juices were flowing and my clit was throbbing. I had gotten so lost in my thoughts of self-gratification that I had forgotten Teddy was even there, until I felt him on top of me.

By this time Teddy was as hard as a wooden stick. His eyes were bulging from his head and the veins in neck were like roots to a tree. His nostrils were stretched and breathing was deep and heavy. He could hardly wait to tear my panties off of me.

No lie after less than 10 pumps it was over. He was getting old. Cum juice was everywhere. I got my money, took a hot shower, put on my floral dress, and put the extra joints in my purse and headed out the door. When I was out the door he yelled at me, "When will I see you again?"

I replied, "At church on Sunday Bye, Pastor Teddy Smith."

Tabernacle...

Chapter 1
In the Beginning

I am Stacey, a beautiful, teasing tan in color, girl from Louisiana. In fact, the actual city of my birth is Algiers, just outside of New Orleans. The distance was so close and Algiers was so small and unpopular, it made perfect sense to say I was born in New Orleans. As far back as I can remember, I have always had quite a bubbly personality. Though I am somewhat guarded with strangers, I love people. I was number two of three children born to Sam and Ebony. I had an older brother, Sam, Jr. and Aston was the baby boy. Our family's birthplace is Louisiana, and although I was a young country girl with that bubbling personality, I still considered my life to be somewhat of a sheltered one.

My parents believed in hard work. My mother was a teacher, and my father was a contractor/construction worker. They later opened a nightclub that was very successful. Every week there was some famous jazz singer, burlesque dancer or zydeco band selling out the club. Sam later invested his money and bought Clip's Barber Shop, Trinity Baptist Church, and unbeknownst to Momma, The Peep Hole.

The Peep Hole was a hotel on Madison Street. The hotel had about 15 rooms and in each room was a woman willing to perform any sexual act for a nominal fee. The Peep Hole was a "whore house" and Samuel Morrison, my daddy, was a pimp. He had no real time to spend with us. You see, daddy was "bad" as hell. He had all kinds of money rolling in. Momma was the best-dressed teacher in St. Landry Parish and we were the best-dressed children in the school.

I attended Phyllis Wheatley High School in Melville, J. S. Clark Elementary School in Opelousas, and Paul L. Dunbar Middle

School in Washington (all in Louisiana) before relocating to Los Angeles, California. All the schools named above were named in honor of someone Black and famous. The elementary and high schools were located in the same immediate vicinity; that's just how small the towns were. The campuses were not attached, and they were all separated by a football field or the band room. Elementary students were not allowed on the high school campus and vice versa.

When I was in elementary school, Mary, my maternal grandma, would get up at 4:00 a.m., get on her knees besides the bed where I slept with her and fervently pray:

Lord, thank you for another day.
Lord, thank you for the roof over our heads.
Hmmm, Oh Lord, have mercy on my family.
Bless 'em throughout this day; give them traveling mercy.
Thank you for the food on our table,
Thank you for the clothes on all our backs,
Thank you for the sunshine well as your rain.

Then she would moan the song:
Oh Lord, have mercy. Have mercy on my soul!

There were stacks of pillows on the bed where she slept. I would peep between the pillows and watch her pray. Sometimes, I would be awakened by Grandma Mary's prayers, crying, and moaning. At the end of the prayer, she would say, "Thank you, Lord, 'cause I knows you heard my prayer."

Mary was a chocolate brown, heavy set, dominating woman that protected her family. She grew up as an only child and she was a young widow, with six children (three girls and three boys.) She wore an apron all the time with her gun in the pocket (kind of resplendent of a modern-day Madea.) She was that loving grandma that would tell you stories, bake you tea cakes, make good pecan candy and potato pies. Mary's mother, my great grandmother (Evelyn, known as Ma Ma) also lived in the house with us. All I remember of her is that she had snow white hair, no teeth and big bow legs. She was bossy. She called her daughter "Boo." All three of Mary's daughters lived in the house: my momma, Ebony, Aunt Gina, and Aunt Kathy. They all were educators.

Between Momma and Aunt Gina, they put a great big bow in my hair every morning. I had the biggest, prettiest ribbon on the top of my head each day. They dressed me in a big can-can slip under a pretty little frilly dress to match my bow with white bobby socks and black and white oxfords. Sam, Jr. wore blue jeans, a matching shirt, and white socks and black and white oxfords.

Grandma Mary would cook a full course breakfast of hot cheesy grits, fresh scrambled eggs from the hens in the back yard, hot crisp bacon, and toast glazed with butter and jelly that she made from her fig tree. She would proceed to call Sam, Jr. and me, "Get up, wash your face, brush your teeth, wash your bodies and come on eat your breakfast. It's time to go to school." I would always go first, but Sam, Jr. would dress our baby brother, Aston. We would sit together at the table and Grandma Mary would say, "Bow your head and bless your food."

"God is great, God is good. Let us thank Him for our food. Bow our heads we must be fed, Give us, Lord, our daily bread. In Jesus' name, Amen." We ate until Aunt Gina would beckon us with a hearty, "Let's go." Sam, Jr. and I would get up and go. Aston was too young; Sam, Jr. was seven, I was three and Aston was a baby. He stayed home with Ma Ma and Grandma Mary, and they spoiled him all day.

Aunt Gina was a high school English teacher at Phyllis Wheatley High School, which was about 64 miles round trip. When we got to school, people thought that Sam, Jr. and I were Aunt Gina's children. Aunt Gina left with us first. Aunt Kathy taught business education in Eunice, which was about 24 miles round trip and Momma left last. She taught elementary school in Plaisance, which was about 12 miles round trip. I thought Aunt Kathy was sooooooo cool. She was my mom's youngest sibling. She let us do silly things and laugh. She would keep us from getting whippings by hiding us. Aunt Kathy actually lived with us in our home in Baton Rouge and attended Southern University.

A typical day started around 5:00 a.m., which is when we would leave Grandma Mary's home. My Aunt Gina shared the driving with two of her co-workers. They would meet us on highway 190 and leave their car in a safe parking spot.

When Aunt Gina said something she meant it. Sam, Jr. and I usually slept all the way after we finished eating. Some mornings it was so foggy, you could hardly see your hand in front of you. By the grace of God and Grandma Mary's prayers, we made it. Sam, Jr. would go to his class and I would go to mine.

At Phyllis Wheatley School, I stayed in the first grade class from the time I was three up until I was five with Ms. Johnson. The little old lady was skinny and tan in color. She wore long dresses below her knees, and because she wore her eye glasses on her nose, she looked over the glasses when talking. At the end of the school year, her students went on to the second grade but Ms. Johnson said I was much too young to move on. I ended up staying in mean old Ms. Johnson's class for three years before she decided to move me into the second grade.

In my class, we prayed, we sung:
Good morning to you, good morning to you.
We were all in our places
With sun shining faces,
For this is the way
To start a new day!

Oh yes, we loved to start each new day with songs, our ABC's:
A B C D E F G H I J K Ella
Minna P
Q R S T U V W X Y & Z
Now I said my ABC's.
Tell me what you think of meeeeeeeeeeeeeeeeeee!

For our counting song, we counted all the way to 100 and memorized a Bible verse from the Psalms. Every morning we screamed "The Lord's Prayer" and "The Pledge of Allegiance." We sang "My Country Tis of Thee" or "God Bless America." We had spelling words that we had to know and use to make up a story. We ate lunch, had naptime, sharing time, and every night we received homework, even on weekends.

When school was out, I would go to Aunt Gina's class and sit in the big chair, starting on my homework until she cleared her room, making sure everything was ready for the next day. Most of the time, I tried to do my homework, but I almost always fell asleep until I was awakened to get out of the car. After school activities, such as dances, basketball games and May Day meant that Aunt Gina would take us to dinner. She would stop by a hotel so we could freshen up or on occasion, a parent would invite us over to eat and to freshen up at their house.

When we arrived home, Grandma Mary had a full course dinner ready. After we ate, it was TV time. We watched our favorite programs like "Popeye" on a black and white set with the two big knobs on the right side and a rabbit ears antenna. There were only three stations so I guess not having a remote was a big thing; you actually had to get up and change the channel. We were so proud to have that old set. Back then having a TV in your house was a big thing, and we were glad that Popeye taught Sam, Jr., Aston and I to eat spinach.

Some evenings after Momma had checked our homework, she and Aunt Kathy would say, "Let's go for a ride." We would jump in the car and go to this club owned by a large family way out in the country. We would all sit in the car in the back of the club and eat Boudin links and drink Cokes. Children were not allowed inside but Momma would take us just to get out of the house. The club did not have restrooms; instead, there were two tall wooden little stalls with a round hole to use on the outside. It was an old time outhouse with no way to flush this outlet, making for a really stinky situation.

There were familiar faces rushing out of the club to the restrooms. Sometimes the lines were long, and this would cause women to run to the men's side. Other women would just go and squat on the side of the club, showing, what I felt was no dignity at all. We would always get home before 8:00 p.m. because if we didn't, Grandma Mary would fuss at Momma and Aunt Kathy for having us out late.

By the time I was in third grade, Momma thought it would be better for me and my brothers to attend the neighborhood school. We could walk to school, participate in school activities and be closer to home. This didn't bother us at all; we were happy. Aston, Sam, Jr., and I walked on the dirt road filled with rocks on Blanchard Street until we got to Jefferson turning left unto the black tar paved streets.

Our new school was J. S. Clark Elementary School. Music was our thing at J. S. Clark. Sam, Jr. and I both played B flat clarinets. Sam also played an alto saxophone and I played the xylophone and the piano. We were in the marching band and the concert band, which allowed us to participate in many parades. This also presented the opportunity for us to compete with other schools in other cities. We proudly wore our J. S. Clark uniforms during halftime at our football games. For us halftime was our show time. We got to go to after school activities including dances, sports and other special programs.

Opelousas had a "Miss Opelousas" contest, and I participated. It was very competitive. I'm glad Momma had exposed me to activities that helped nurture my talents. She had invested in private piano lessons. So, for the talent part of the contest, I played a musical piece by Beethoven. I placed 1st in the competition, but I was not the queen. I just could not understand, especially after I knew I had done my very best. I was so sad.

I also liked to dance. "The Slop" and the "Mashed Potatoes" were popular dances when I was coming up. The Mashed Potatoes was so popular there was a song named after it: "Do the mashed potato, yeah, yeah, yeah!" The Mashed Potatoes was a lot of fun, but I was the queen of "doing the Slop." At any given time or place, I would hear The Mashed Potatoes or The Slop Song and I would start dancing. You should have seen me in my bobby socks and black and white oxfords!

During my elementary school years, attendance was a very important in my home. I was brought up and taught to believe that attendance meant self-discipline, and that it would give a good indication on how one's life would turn out. All of the adults in my life who had jobs were always at work.

My eighth grade graduation was very memorable. The girls had to wear white pleated skirts, white blouses with a burgundy tie and white patent leather shoes. The boys wore dark dress pants, white shirts and burgundy ties. As homely as I looked, I was very honored to have achieved perfect attendance for eight years. I also won the All-around Female Student award and I was an honor roll student. I participated in the chorus, marching band, 4-H Club, Girl Scouts, speech and drama clubs and Junior Leadership. My momma, Grandma Mary, my brothers, and aunts were always there for me during my school days.

Sam, Jr. and I had a good relationship while we were in elementary and junior high. The summer he got chicken pox, I cried to get them also because I wanted him to share them with me. In a little girl's eyes Sam, Jr. was the big brother and I just adored him. He was actually the big brother that everyone just loved. Junior had a cream color complexion and hazel green eyes. He was tall and handsome.

I looked at my brother as the green-eyed monster that could get away with everything. I remember when we attended Phyllis Wheatley School in Melville, he felt like he needed to be the class clown, which landed him in a lot of trouble one day. He told this rhyme to his classmates, "Motorboat, motorboat. Go so fast. Motorboat, motorboat. Kick them in the a—."

I was so scared for him. My heart was racing so fast because I just knew the teachers, my Aunt Gina and Momma were going to kill my big brother. The teacher did whip him and took him straight to Aunt Gina who, by the way, was also Junior's Godmother, but that didn't really matter. Grown folks just did not accept children being disrespectful and when Sam, Jr. got in trouble my heart would beat fast for him.

Sam, Jr., Aston, Momma and I only stayed in Opelousas during the week. We went home on the weekends. I was happy on the way home playing and fighting with my two brothers, but at the same time, I was a little girl not wanting to be at home in Baton Rouge. I feared Daddy's voice. I would shiver every time he called me or my brothers; it was always a scream. He did not know how to talk in a normal voice. Oh, my God! How he would yell and curse at Momma. After all, Sam was the man. Sometimes she would just start praying loud or start repeating passages from the 23rd Psalms, "The Lord is my shepherd, I shall not want," or Psalm 121, "I will lift up mine eyes to the hills from whence cometh my help. My help cometh from the Lord which made heaven and earth."

Momma took this for a long time. She did not realize how it affected me. As we grew older and the verbal abuse was still happening, Aston and Sam, Jr. challenged Daddy. They were not going to allow Daddy to keep screaming and hollering at Momma. Sam, Jr. would say, "Don't holler at my momma." In return, Daddy would yell obscenities at him. Aston was small, but that didn't stop him from talking a lot of trash about what he was going to do. I was scared and would start crying. I would go in the living room and call my uncle, my mother's brother, who was a minister. He did not live far away, and sometimes he would call back to talk to Momma. I never understood why she would always say everything was OK.

This occurred for many years. When we would get to Baton Rouge, Momma would wait on Daddy like he was a king. She fixed his bath water, she cooked dinner and she ate at the table with us while Daddy waited in the bed for her to bring him his dinner on a tray. She washed and ironed his clothes, yet all we ever heard from him was grumbling. We knew not to disturb him or we would be yelled at. It was really all about him. Daddy would take us to Ervinville, which was south of Baton Rouge, to baseball games. My brother and I sold peanuts in the baseball stand while he drank at the bar. Not one time in my life had Daddy ever told me the words, "I love you," until Christmas of 2007. Believe it or not, that was his last civil conversation before Alzheimer's kicked in.

Aston was very opinionated at an early age. He would say, "No," and he meant every bit of it. Sam, Jr. and I would say, "How high," if Daddy told us to jump, but not Aston. He would say, "No," and would not move. I remember when Aston was only about seven, Daddy attempted to whip him and he grabbed the belt. I was so scared I wet myself and thought, "Has Aston lost his mind?" Guess what? Nothing happened but Daddy cursed him out in his loud screaming voice and let Aston alone.

My paternal grandmother (Ma Bonnie) lived within walking distance from our house in Baton Rouge, which made it easy for Sam, Jr., Aston and I to walk over and visit her. She lived in a little wooden frame three -bedroom house with a big pecan and fig tree in the back yard. My daddy's two brothers had houses on the same lot of land. Whenever we entered Ma Bonnie's nice, clean house, we were always told to be on our best behavior. Everything was always shining, smelling clean and looking unmarked. Her glasses, her floors, her stove were always in top- notch shape.

She always greeted us with a kiss and fed us even if we said, "No, thank you." We looked forward to her milk and cookies. As I recall, we had milk with everything because Ma Bonnie did not believe in giving children sodas.

I watched Ma Bonnie clean, cook, and dress. Everything had to match. Her shoes, purse, gloves and hats were all coordinated. I observed her even ironing tablecloths and sheets. My daddy was totally the opposite of Ma Bonnie. She was quiet, humble and gracious. He was loud and obnoxious.

My mother's brother was a pastor of two churches in Baton Rouge. Reverend Herbert Paul George was a prominent minister. He was known as a good-hearted pastor that helped his members. He had one large church and a small one. Momma, Sam, Jr., Aston and I were members of the small church. Momma actually helped to build our church, Sweet Home Missionary Baptist Church. Momma was in the senior choir, and my brothers and I were in the children's choir.

After going to school all week, we spent Friday afternoons traveling back to Baton Rouge. By evening time, we had to go to choir rehearsal. We had suppers at church with all kinds of good southern food. There was fried fish/fried chicken/chitterlings, with collard greens, potato salad, bread, candied yams and a piece of cake or pie, and you could buy a plate for $3.00. After selling church dinners, Momma would drop us home and go to the bar that my daddy managed. She often stayed until closing, make the payroll and then come home. The bar was right next door to a liquor store. As a matter of fact, you could actually walk through one to get to the other.

On Saturdays, we would go to Ma Bonnie's house or go with Momma back to the church to sell and deliver dinners. We were trying to build a larger church, which we eventually did five years later. On Sundays, we went to Sunday school and church service. We would then go home to eat, then go back to church for BTYU (Baptist Training Youth Union.) There was 6:00 p.m. prayer and 7:30 p.m. night service. When we got home on Sunday nights, we got ready for the next morning back to Opelousas. We looked forward to Momma giving us dinner when we got home. We did not get a chance to see too much of Daddy. He would say he had to work and take care of his club on Gus Young Avenue. Later, I found out this was not the case at all.

Once back in Opelousas, our Wednesday nights were usually spent at the family church, Little Zion Missionary Baptist Church. This is the place where we had Bible Study and prayer meeting. (Sweet Home was my uncle's church.) When we did not go to Little Zion, we met in the living room of our home and had prayer meeting. We sang hymns, read the Bible and prayed. Ma Ma, Grandma Mary and Nana (Aunt Elaine, who was Ma Ma's sister, my great great aunt) would join us. These three old ladies would get on their knees and start praying. They prayed those long, down home feeling prayers. They were so long that we thought they were never going to get up. They would moan and groan and call on the name of Jesus. It was funny to us. We would open our eyes, look at each other and burst out in laughter. Later in life, I came to realize that praying a long time is no joke; it's real. **(You are really telling God how you feel!)**

Little Zion Missionary Baptist Church was one of the largest colored churches in Opelousas. It had its own private cemetery where most of my ancestors are buried. My brothers and I were all baptized at Little Zion.

Grandma Mary's house was a little white-framed house with green trim and a fence around it. We lived there for a long time. Aunt Gina got married in the living room of our home in Baton Rouge

Chapter 2
Family Feud

While Daddy was working his construction business, he was also steadily drinking and spending money on women. He'd often boast about being "The Man." Let him tell it, he was "Big Daddy." It pained my brothers and me that he spent so little time with the three of us. He would come home and argue and fight Momma. All that screaming he did was frightening to me. It bothered my brothers so much that they would scheme about ways to get back at him.

By the time he was 15 or 16, Sam, Jr. organized a band, which consisted of him and his friends. Making music was therapeutic for him; it helped him escape all the madness we experienced at home. He played saxophone, Martin played the guitar, John played the drums and Alvin sang. They practiced hours and hours every day. Sam, Jr. and the band opened most of the shows at the club. He could blow his tail off playing Junior Walker and the All Stars. Jr. was really good, but no matter how good he was, it didn't stop Daddy from calling him derogatory names and speaking down to him: "That big head bastard should be good for something. Come here, boy, and get a drink." Now, my brother was drinking against my mother's wishes and against his upbringing, but he would do anything to get Daddy's attention. I'm so grateful that no matter what Sam, Jr. had to endure in life, he never went to jail.

The Bamboo was the hottest thing going in Opelousas. The club opened around 10:00 a.m. and closed at 3:00 or 4:00 a.m. and it was open seven days a week. You could rest assured we had the best music of the day at the club. One such song was Bobby "Blue" Bland's "The Eagle fly on Friday and Saturday I go out to Play." The music drew people from everywhere. It was so crowded you could not even get in the place. Ko Ko Taylor, BB King and the

Zydeco bands came. Commercials played on the local colored radio stations. I was so excited. "WOW," I thought. "We are rich." It was soooooooooo nice. On Monday nights, Grandma Mary and Momma made tripe fiea, a well-loved and highly popular Cajun dish. Tuesday through Friday, we had happy hour drinks for only $.50. Saturday and Sundays, we had live entertainment. Everything was so cool while we were in the public eye, but at home it was another story because daddy continued to verbally and physically abuse Momma.

Soon business started slacking. The Bamboo Seafood Inn's business went from over 200-300 cars to 10-11 cars. This brought on a tremendous amount of stress to Momma and the entire family. I could see it in Momma's face. She would never say anything negative about Daddy, but we could hear. My heart would pound harder and harder. I wanted to go tell Daddy to leave my Momma alone. I wanted to beat on the door and say, "You know we are right in the next room, crazy man! We can hear you arguing with Momma." Of course, Momma would always tell us, "What goes on in our home stays in our home."

Momma was disrespected by young women she hired as waitresses at the club. Daddy had told them he was the boss, and whatever he said went. According to him, they did not have to listen to Momma.

I even remember one weekend Momma was very sick. In fact, she was so sick she could not even get out of the bed. We were in Baton Rouge. My brothers and I were in the bed because Momma told us to go to bed and look at TV until we fell asleep. Two young pretty females; Yvette and Genetta; that Momma had brought from Plaisance and employed as waitresses at the club in Baton Rouge lived in our family home in the guest room. Late one night, a forty-five record kept playing. The song was, "Baby, I Almost Lost my Mind." The song played over and over and over again, eventually waking up my Momma. Momma got up out of the bed because she thought one of the young pretty waitress females had forgotten and left the record player on. Much to Momma's amazement, Daddy was in the living room with one of the bar maids making out with her. This was not a pretty scene, especially since they were right there in our home. All hell broke loose. Momma was infuriated and she went on a rampage through the living room. My brothers and I were awakened by Daddy's cursing and him trying to protect Daisy, who flew out of the house. Daddy was trying to hold Momma down because I truly believe if he hadn't, Momma could have gotten to Daisy and she would have hurt her real bad. Daddy grabbed Momma from the rear and was holding her.

By then, Sam, Jr., Aston, and I ran from our bedrooms scared to death. I was screaming, Aston was screaming, "Turn my momma loose," and Jr. grabbed Daddy and told him to get his hands off of Momma. The two ladies came out of their bedroom. Neither one of them made any noise. They were just as much in shock as we were. I ran to the bedroom and called my uncle. I was screaming and crying. My uncle told me to calm down. He was on his way over.

It was early in the morning and with all the commotion, the neighbors had come out to see what was going on. My uncle came right over. He tried to calm me down. My brothers were still going back and forth confronting my daddy. Momma was trying to make the boys behave themselves. My uncle settled things down by convincing Daisy to leave our home. He called her a taxi while she continued denying any wrongdoing. She said she was falsely accused and that she was only coming to get her payroll check. Some paycheck! My uncle told Momma to get in the car and take me for ride. "Stacey is very upset. Take her for a ride now," he said. Momma told me try not to cry. We rode in the early morning for about an hour.

When we got back home, Aston, Sam, Jr., Yvette, and Genetta were sitting in the living room. Momma fixed us all some break-fast. It was on a Sunday morning. We got our things ready so we could go to church. After attending church, Momma took us to the movies. All of us were emotionally upset; however, we did not talk to anyone about the incident in the early morning. That Sunday night, daddy started wolfing at Momma again. It appeared that they argued in to the morning. When we got up early Monday morning to head to Opelousas, he took a physical punch at Momma. Sam, Jr. grabbed at him. Again, I was in my emotional state screaming and crying. Momma hit daddy with something and I saw blood. Boy, did I really have a fit! We left while Sam, Jr. stayed and helped Daddy repair himself. At first, I couldn't believe Sam, Jr. stayed with him, but then I remember that he was that kind of a person. He would talk a lot of crap but he had a heart of gold.

On the way to Opelousas, Momma made Aston and I promise not to say anything to Grandma Mary. We complied. Grandma Mary was a wise old lady though. She knew something was wrong when Sam, Jr. was not with us. All the drama ran Yvette and Genatta away. One of them went back home to live and the other one rented her own apartment in Baton Rouge.

As time went on, business continued to go down. Momma started stressing and looking like someone was beating her down. It was the end of summer 1967, and Daddy was singing words from the famous Temptations' song:

I know you wanna leave me but I refuse to let you go.
If I have to beg and plead for your sympathy,
I don't mind 'cause you mean that much to me.
Ain't too proud to beg.

But about two months later, Momma packed up and left us with a heavy heart. She prayed and shed tears. She had been disrespected. Enough was enough. She told us she was going to California to help better our lives. She needed a new start. She left on the Greyhound bus.

I missed our routine. Now, I had to stay with Grandma Mary. During this time, I had a boyfriend. It seemed like Andre was the only one I could talk to about all the crap that was going on in my life. It surely didn't feel good. Andre lived in a rural part of Washington, Louisiana. I was elated when my homeroom teacher, Dr. Brown, agreed to allow me to ride with him to and from school. Grandma Mary paid him bi-weekly for gas. Because of Dr. Brown, I got to see my boyfriend on a regular basis.

Andre was 6' 2" and good looking. Tan in color, he was the apple of my eye. In our young love, we promised each other that we would be together for the rest of our lives. Looking back, I wonder how we could lie to each other when we were so young. On weekends, he would get up at the crack of dawn and dig worms for a fisherman, who would pay him. With that money, he would catch a taxi to come and see me. We would sit and look at the big black and white TV in the family room with Grandma Mary and Sheila. Grandma Mary would relax every evening with her Bible in her hand, her gun in her apron pocket, and blue foot tub filled with hot water, Epson salt and olive oil.

After I would heat the water on the stove and pour it in the old rusty tub for Grandma, Andre and I would wait until she would place her feet in the water and we would exit to the sitting room across from the family room. We would put the forty-five records on the record player and listen to music. We would dance on fast songs like, "Who Will Take the Lady with the Skinny Legs?" by Joe Tex, "Green Onions" by Booker T & the MG's, and James Brown's, "I Feel Good." We would fast dance until we were sweating. We would laugh and have a good time.

If only I could have put that point in my life on pause it would have been fine with me. But as things turned out, I had to face the harsh reality that all good things must soon come to an end.

Chapter 3

Exodus: From Louisiana to California

I was now 15-years-old and as happy as I possibly could be. I had Andre to help ease the burdens of what I was experiencing at home. I woke up one day with this empty spot in my heart, and I realized Momma was not there anymore for me to call on or depend on. If only she could be here when I needed her for any and every thing. I felt her absence every day. And not that it mattered much, but my daddy was physically out of my life, too.

Thank God Grandma Mary was still there for me, but it was not the same as having Momma there. About one year later, Grandma woke me up and told me, "You are going to meet your mother. You are getting too womanish." What had I done to make her feel this way? Why now? School would soon be over. I thought everything was alright. I talked to Momma every day. What was wrong? I was trying to adjust to Grandma's strictness, but I guess I was not adjusting fast enough. I had heard and read so much about California, but for me to leave Grandma Mary and my comfort zone brought butterflies to my stomach.

Every day, Dr. Brown picked me up and brought me home to Grandma's big house, which seemed almost empty since everybody was practically gone. Aunt Kathy, Aunt Gina, Aston, and Momma were already in California and it looked like I was headed there too. Sam, Jr. was in the United States Marines and stationed in El Toro, California.

Grandma's words had come to pass. I found myself on an airplane traveling to Los Angeles, California. I had heard about the big city, but living there would prove to be another story. I didn't know what to expect. Would I meet new friends? Would I get lost amidst all the big buildings? Most importantly, what would it be like entering a new school so close to the time for me to graduate from high school?

It was a beautiful day when the airplane landed in Los Angeles. Because this was my first time flying, I was really scared so I prayed. And although I wanted to see and to be with my momma, I couldn't help but feel the void in my life from being separated from Andre.

When the plane landed, Momma and Aunt Gina met me at the airport. As it was customary for our family, we hugged and kissed during our reunion. We were so happy to see each other. Momma took me on a short tour on our way home. I still couldn't believe I was in Los Angeles. I was so afraid of the change of atmosphere that I still had butterflies in my stomach.

We arrived to our new home on Normandie Avenue, and Momma showed me my room. She also showed me her room, which was in the rear of the house. The room assignment brought about some startling news. I would have a roommate. This was a major adjustment because having a roommate was something totally new to me. I didn't like this idea, but there was nothing I could do about it. This roommate was a girl about my age, who also had a brother that lived in the house with Momma. I had to let Momma know that I would be spending a lot of time in her room because the idea of having a roommate, especially one I did not know, just didn't sit right with me.

Momma showed me around the huge house. It had four big bedrooms, a large living room, dining room, kitchen and a break-fast room off from the kitchen, a service porch and two bathrooms. It was different from the other homes I had lived in. My younger auntie who had been living in California for a while lived right around the corner. After Momma instructed me on how to get there, I walked over to see her. I was afraid, but still, I went. As I passed along, I spoke to people, but I was in total shock when they did not speak back. They looked at me as if I was an alien. I felt really strange. I thought, "Have I done something wrong?" Then I realized it wasn't me. It was this place - which I previously thought was paradise on earth had strange people; people different from me.

People living here didn't speak to strangers. This was odd for me because I had been taught to speak to everyone.

When I got to my auntie's house, I was very happy. We used to talk on the telephone all the time when I was in Louisiana. She was real upbeat, and I liked her very much. We talked and laughed about everything. We had a very good day. Momma came and met me at her house and then we walked home.

One of my biggest concerns about relocating to California was what I would do about school. Well, school was still in session when I arrived in California. Momma was teaching in Compton during the day, and she taught in Los Angeles at Washington Adult School two nights a week. On the weekends, she also worked at White Front Store. I have to admit that Momma was a workaholic. She wanted the best for my brothers and me. I went with her a few days on her day job. I was very inquisitive and wanted to know where I would attend school, if I would be graduating, and if the school would accept the credits I had already earned in Louisiana. Would I be able to get a job? Would Andre still come to see me?

I finally met the brother of my roommate; his name was Jaray. He was attending school and held an evening job. Momma introduced me to him, and later, he asked me to go on a date to the drive-in movies. I remember talking to Andre, but already the distance had started to change our relationship. He had given me an engagement ring before I left, but within three months of me arriving in California, I sent it back. I can't remember if I did so voluntarily or if he asked for it back. At any rate, I sent it back. Soon after that, I heard that he was getting married. My feelings were hurt, but I got over it. Of course, I had also gone on a date with my roommate's brother, Jaray, so I really couldn't have been too hurt.

In June 1968, I wanted a job so badly. Everyone in the house was motivated and had jobs. I applied for a summer youth program. At the time, it was called the National Youth Corp. (NYC). I passed the test allowing me to be accepted into the program. Thank God, I passed. As a result, I ended up working for the IRS in downtown Los Angeles. My mother would drop me off and pick me up. Because Driver's Education was a requirement in the Opelousas schools, I already knew how to drive. This made it easy for me to ask Momma to take me to get my driver's license. I had even learned how to drive a four-speed. My only problem and fear was driving in Southern California. Well, I got my license and Momma let me drive her Pontiac Lemans.

My momma was very proud of me. I earned my own money and I was looking forward to my senior year in this big city. I was intimidated by my surroundings, but I was ready to take on this new challenge. Momma enrolled me in Manual Arts High School, the nearby high school. They checked my records from Louisiana and found I had enough credits to graduate in one semester. All I had to do was take three required courses. The principal was concerned about me graduating at sixteen because he said I was immature. I'm so glad Momma didn't go for that crap. She told him she felt I could handle it.

I had a very nice counselor, Ms. Pamela Williams, who helped me when I encountered a problem getting a required class. The history classes were filled, so I enrolled in a night school class. The late Ms. Georgia Miller was my teacher. She had me so scared that I was not going to pass her class that I studied very hard and did extra work so I could graduate.

My roommate, her brother and I all attended the same school, and we all got closer. My roommate had a boyfriend, and after awhile, Jaray and I started to date. He had four classes, and in the afternoon he went to work. His work experience counted as a class. We went on a few dates. He had a car, so occasionally I rode with him to school. He was a senior too, and we graduated together. He had print shop classes, so he made our class graduation invitations. I graduated with a 3.9 grade point average, which put me in the top 10% of the last winter class at Manual Arts High School. I received a silver-seal medal for my accomplishments at 16-years old.

As a result of my scholastic achievement, I received a full, four-year scholarship to the University of Evanston, Illinois, a scholarship at Spelman, and one at Howard, but I didn't want to go; I was afraid to leave. I cried and told Momma she was just trying to get rid of me. Also, after losing my first boyfriend by moving to

California, I didn't want to lose my new friend by relocating again. I had just started dating this young man. If I knew later what I would come to know about Jaray, I wouldn't have pitched such a fit. Jaray later became my husband. We had a stressful marriage but I praise God that the relationship produced three wonderful children. Nonetheless, Momma gave in and told me I didn't have to leave.

After graduation, I had no intentions of going anywhere. My momma, however, had another plan in mind. She told me there was a college in Compton (the city where she worked) and that I was going to go to a school somewhere. Without a fuss, I enrolled in Compton Junior College, along with my boyfriend, Jaray. I was told college was a little more difficult than high school, but I was not intimidated. I spoke to a counselor, got my schedule of classes and started school.

As time went on, the relationship between my momma and daddy grew worse, and they eventually divorced. Sam, Sr. was still living his life and not supporting Sam, Jr., Aston and me. During the time between high school graduation and starting college, Momma married Isaiah North. My stepfather is deceased now, but he was really a wonderful man. He bought me my first car. When he and Momma bought a three-bedroom home in Compton, we all moved (me, Momma, Isaiah and Aston). I loved our new home. I had my own bedroom. Aston and Sam, Jr. shared whenever Sam, Jr. was home from the military. The bedrooms had intercoms. I remember my brothers would wake up very early, and wake me up by calling me out my name over the intercom.

I went to school and worked at Sears on Vermont and Slauson in Los Angeles. Jaray and I continued to date. After attending Compton Junior College one semester, I then enrolled at Pepperdine College in August of that same year. I planned to get out of school quickly by attending both colleges. I was now 17-years-old. I took 30-36 units a trimester/semester. I was a smart girl with a determination to become an educator.

By the age of 20, I had earned an Associate's degree from Compton and a Bachelor's degree from Pepperdine and began teaching at

Bethune Junior High School. By that time, I had also gotten married to Jaray. To our dismay, our union was not one of wedded bliss. To make matters worse, two years later after arriving in Los Angeles, my life as a pastor's mistress and madam would begin. If I could have turned back the hands of time, I surely would have done things differently. While I couldn't change my dreaded fate at the time, I can tell you how I landed in this foreign land and how, by the grace of God, I was delivered. Little did I know that my exodus from Louisiana to California would be more like an excursion from a plateau of peace to a plunge into the Lion's den. The journey continues.

Chapter 4

Truly the Lord is in This Place...Well, at Least That's What I Thought

One glad morning when this life is over, I'll fly away.
Oh, oh, oh, I'll fly away, oh glory.
I'll fly away.
When I die, hallelujah by and by.
I'll fly away.

When I arrived in Southern California, I discovered that my family had not abandoned its tradition of attending church on a regular basis. The words to the song, "I'll Fly Away," resonate in my head until this very day. My family had joined a large missionary Baptist church. It was natural for me to attend and join shortly thereafter. As the members of the congregation joined in with the man who was leading the song, I noticed that he had the whole church leaning and rocking. I slowly walked in innocently, not knowing I was going into the lion's den. The man who was singing was the associate pastor. I had no clue that I would eventually end up being his mistress and the madam for his pastor-friends of large congregations.

I must admit that there was nothing physically attractive about this man. He was a giant looking monstrous man who stood about 6' 5". With a huge head and a short haircut, he very much resembled the combination of a bulldog and a large football player ready to do a tackle. He swayed back and forth singing with such emotion until sisters in the church were shouting all over the place. The organist played as long as he sang. It was a sight to behold. Momma and I walked in. She was very excited about having me by her side once again in church and I was elated.

The choir sang, the deacons prayed, and then another huge dark man dressed in a robe got up and prayed, "Lord, thank you for another opportunity to be here. I ask that you decrease me and increase you. In Jesus' name I pray, amen."

I leaned over and asked Momma, "Who is that?"

She said, "He's the pastor of this church."

"Well, who was that other man that was singing," I asked.

She responded, "Be quiet, girl. We are in church."

I sat back, looked and listened.

I did not join church that Sunday, but the very next one, I did. I had this size 0 junior petite navy blue suit on with navy blue nylon stockings and black leather pump shoes. My hair was shoulder length and I thought I was "Miss Thang" that day.

The associate minister said it was customary to invite those who did not have a church home or those wishing to be baptized to come down and be his special guest on the front row. The deacons would stand and extend their arms and the ushers would escort the people to the front row. "Okay, here I go," I said to myself. I walked down the aisle and sat on the front seat. A woman in the choir came up and sang a solo. The pastor proceeded to do his prayer, the sermon, and then opened the doors of the church while the associate minister sang:

Beams of heaven as I go
Through the wilderness below
Guide my feet in peaceful ways
Turn my midnights into days.
(Chorus) I do not know how long 'twill be
Nor what the future holds for me.
But this I know, if Jesus leads me
I shall get home some day.

He sung the chorus over and over. Women were passing out, some were shouting, some were jumping and hollering, "Hallelujah." Hats were falling, shoes were coming off, women were just lying out still on the floor and ushers were rushing to cover their pretty legs. The pastor, associate ministers, ushers, and deacons had their extended arms for the unsaved to get saved and the ones with no church home to come up. The offer was also for the ones who wanted to rededicate their lives to the Lord to come forth. There I was. I ran up there and joined the church. I wanted a church home. I wanted to belong to the same church as my family. I had no clue whatsoever that this was not such a good thing.

After I joined the church, I was taken out of the sanctuary by a hospitality committee. They prayed with me and told me about the different organizations/auxiliaries that were available to me. I joined the teenage choir. I went to practices faithfully in my quest to be a good choir member. I attended Sunday school faithfully. But after only a short period of being a member at the church, there was some kind of split up within the church. I kept going there until I finally decided to go check out the other church. When I did, I saw that it was "on and poppin'," as the young people would say.

The church was crowded. The associate minister from the church I had joined was now the pastor of this church. The choir was singing, people were shouting, and people were coming from all parts of the city. The church was very crowded for all three services. (We had services at 7:00 and 11:00 a.m., and also at 7:00 p.m.) There were so many people in the church that they eventually had to add on to the building.

In an effort to assure that everyone was accommodated, the ushers had to place chairs down the aisle. There was constantly a plea for tithes, offerings, building fund monies, and offerings for the pastor's aide and his love offerings. Soon, Pastor had built himself a fabulous penthouse, which I later referred to as The Lion's Den. In it, he had a dressing room, bathroom, plush carpet, a pullout sofa bed, a large desk and a private secretary that sat right out from his closed double door office. He had cameras and videos in his large private office. He knew who was there and could scope the congregation before he ever came into the sanctuary.

As I continued to attend services there, I observed notes being handed by deacons and ushers to Pastor while he was in the pulpit and he would glance at them. When he would get up, he would be singing, which he did very well. Then, just before he would pray, he would announce, "It's prayer time." Members and friends of the congregation would all run up with sincere hearts and come and leave their burdens at the altar. As we gathered around the altar, Pastor would come up and start singing:

Amazing Grace will always be my song of praise.
For it was grace that bought my liberty.
I'll never know just how He came to love me so.
He looked beyond my faults and saw my needs.

By the time Pastor had gotten to the second time singing the chorus, people would be screaming throughout the church. I remember once he said, "That song was a special request from Sister Jones, and today, we are praying for the following:" His momma would always be at the top of the list. He would pray for those on the sick list, those in the hospital and at home, the bereaved families and all members and visiting friends. He prayed for a long time. When he finished, it was if the people's burdens really had been removed. He had a voice that sounded better than Barry White or Luther Vandross.

A few Sundays passed. I eventually joined the church. Not one for being a pew warmer, I joined the teenage choir and attended Sunday school. I had gone to Bible Study and choir rehearsals faithfully. Pastor had a huge church but I was surprised that he came out to the Bible Study and to choir rehearsals when I attended. I was even more amazed that he knew his members. He knew just who I was and he knew all of my family members. That was amazing to me, especially considering the size of his large congregation.

As I continued coming to church, I discovered that there was more to the building than the sanctuary. Before you got upstairs to the private secretary and his office, there were bar doors that easily put you in the mind of entering The President's Suite. If that wasn't enough, anyone entering had to go through the security/body guard before you got to him. How do I know? Because I had the privileges to go up there anytime I desired to see him before service or even after service. All I had to do was make a telephone call to his private line where he answered himself. He knew to tell all personnel that I just described to let me in without any questions.

I attended church faithfully, just as I had at the previous church. I was so glad to have found a new church home, a place where I could worship God and grow spiritually. I was looking forward to giving the Lord the best of my service, but just as any young girl who was "cute and smart," I let my looks go to my head. I didn't know it, but just by being myself, I was a target. I was young, intelligent and attractive. I did not come from such a strict upbringing that my style of dress was guarded. So, as a young girl, I took advantage of the privilege of wearing clothes that showed my figure. Neither my momma nor I saw any harm in this. As time went on, though, just being me ended up being more than I ever dreamed of bargaining for.

Chapter 5

Subliminal Seduction

I will never forget the time I received a telephone call that changed me for the rest of my young adult life. During my first year in college, I received a call that requested me to come to a church meeting at a hotel. Now, where I come from, this was not a strange request; it was very commonplace for churches to have meetings at hotels. Plus, my momma and my stepfather trusted me. I was mature for my age and I had never given them any problems.

Since I had gotten my driver's license, my stepfather bought me a cute little 1968 dark blue Volkswagen when I graduated from high school. I was so crazy about it. I took it to be my pride and joy. These were the days that the hippies were very popular. I was not a hippy but I placed love flowers on my car and referred to it as "My Love Bug." Gas was only about 30 cents a gallon. I thought I was all of that and a bag of chips. I had begun college, had my own job and could ride when I got ready. So, when the telephone call came in, it was no big deal.

One Saturday around 12:00 noon, the telephone rang. Momma and Daddy were sitting down talking to me. We were at home just relaxing and enjoying each other's company. I jumped up and answered the telephone.

"Hello?" There was a long pause, so I said, "Hell——-o?"

A male's voice spoke and said, "May I speak to **Stacey?**"

"Yes, this is **Stacey**. Who did you say was calling?" I responded.

He said, "This is Jacob. I'm calling for Pastor Smith. He wants to know if you can come to a meeting today at 6:00 p.m. at the LAX Hilton."

I said, "Yes. What is this meeting pertaining to? Should I dress casual, dressy or formal?"

Jacob said, "Just dress casual."

I explained to him I did not know my way around L.A. and he relayed the message to Pastor. Jacob told me to be ready and someone would pick me up.

I said, "Okay."

He said, "Okay," and we hung up.

When I hung up, I innocently told Momma and Daddy I had to go to a church meeting and I was going to be picked up and brought back home. Momma said, "Okay." Later, I showered, dressed, and waited to be picked up by Jacob.

It was about 5:30 p.m. when a shiny black limo pulled up to our home. Jacob walked up to the door and rang the bell. I looked through the peephole and said, "Yes?"

A deep male's voice came from the other end, "Miss Stacey, are you ready?"

I was dressed in a black two-piece suit with a black halter top, fish net stockings and black pump shoes. I took a pen and a notebook with me so I could take good notes from the meeting.

Jacob opened the car door for me and I got into this plush leather seat in the rear. Just sitting in the car made it impossible for me to not inhale and exhale very slowly. Being naive, I said to myself, "Wow, what did I do to deserve all of this luxury?" He had soft music playing from 94.7 The Wave, a popular station in L.A. I did not say anything nor did he.

You may wonder how in the world my parents allowed me to leave the house in a stretch limo without asking any questions. Well, the way my parents' house was built made it difficult for them to see what I left in. Our house was surrounded by a white picket fence, and it sat back a good distance away from the street. I was already expecting Jacob, so naturally, I answered the door. After all, you must remember that my parents did not baby me. They trusted me to do what I said I was going to do. Plus, I had never given them a reason to not trust me, and as far as they knew, there was no reason to be suspecting. I was simply going to a church meeting. That's all.

When Jacob drove into the underground parking of the LAX Hilton to valet parking, the door was opened for me. A gentleman in a uniform reached for my hand and I exited the car. He took the car and Jacob and I walked in revolving doors with large chandeliers hanging from the ceiling. There was a huge fountain with water flowing in streams. A man was sitting at this baby grand black piano playing soft jazz music. I was looking around all of this beautiful scenery and walked behind Jacob toward the elevator. I felt like Dorothy in "The Wizard of Oz." He pushed the elevator door going up. When we got in the elevator he pushed the button for the 22nd floor and we got out. He then used some type of card to go to the penthouse. I was thinking, "Wow, what kind of meeting was this going to be?"

We got to the room and knocked on the door once; then he used a room key. My heart was thumping. I thought, "Okay, why are we going to a room?" When the door opened, I was in a state of shock. I could not believe my eyes. Not only was my pastor, Reverend Smith, sitting in the plush suite drinking liquor, which included half of gallons of Smirnoff Vodka, Tanqueray Gin, Hennessey, Cognac, Budweiser Beer and Old Fosterer Bourbon with chasers (Coke, 7-up, tonic water), but he was also sitting there listening to BB King's "I'll Play the Blues for you."

What a strange scene! Unfortunately, that wasn't the worst part. When I got in and looked around, I was totally shocked to find that there were several well-known pastors of large congregations doing likewise. The room had two king size beds, a large sofa and it was joined to another room which not only had a sofa but a bar. I felt out of place and misled. It was awkward and I had butterflies in my stomach. This was a man I respected and looked up to regarding my religious beliefs. He had been teaching The Ten Commandments, about adultery, fornication, what is expected from us to see the kingdom of heaven and other scriptural lessons. I never in a million years thought I would see this from him. This was so very contrary to his teachings.

After I thought about it, I said to myself, "Oh, my God! I have placed this man on a pedestal." Oh, how I enjoyed him preaching and singing. Now I felt deceived. I asked why I was there with a room full of men. I wanted to know where the meeting was. Pastor Smith looked at me with big red eyes, opening and closing them and patting his hands together. He licked his lips and replied, "Well, daughter, you are a chosen one. Consider yourself 'cream of the crop.' This is our meeting."

I thought, "What on God's earth have I gotten myself into? **What does he mean cream of the crop?**" I never asked or bargained for that. As I looked around the room, I said, "Reverend Stevens, Reverend Joseph and Reverend Jenkins, you are doing this, too?" I was in dismay. After all, we fellowshipped with their churches.

They thought it was funny and laughed, "Welcome to the meeting."

Reverend Joseph said, "She's a pretty young thing, Doc."

Reverend Smith looked up with his glossy, drunken eyes and said, "I know. Hands off. She belongs to me."

Jacob did not say a word. Pastor Smith patted his leg and said, "Come sit here," pointing to his knee. I slowly came over to him not knowing what to expect. He stuck his tongue in my ear and whispered, "This is between us. No one is to know about this at all. Do you understand?"

Not knowing what to expect, I softly said, "Okay."

He stopped talking and starting kissing me over my cheek and neck. I remember how the feel of his wet sloppy lips felt nasty. Yet, I did not mutter a word. I was as scared as I could be, and I hoped this so called meeting would soon be over. I asked myself, "What's next?"

Reverend Smith asked me to look on the menu and order anything I wanted to eat and drink.

Nervously, I agreed. I ordered the prime rib well done, a baked potato with butter, sour cream, and chives, and a tossed green salad with ranch dressing. He ordered the same thing but with a different type of dressing. We ate. The other pastors were steadily drinking with their shoes off and listening to eight track tapes of Marvin Gaye, Teddy Pendergrass and Aretha Franklin.

That night he ordered white zinfandel for me and I drank a glass. We sat at the table, and it felt like the wine went straight to my head. I was feeling real loose and relaxed. "Are you okay," he whispered in my ear. I couldn't believe it. There I was drinking at seventeen years old with my pastor who was thirteen years older than me. I shook my head and said, "Yes."

He then took his tongue and licked my neck and stuck his tongue in my ear. The sensations caused me to become wet in my panties, but it wasn't liquid from urine. This made me scared as hell. Then all of a sudden he just stopped abruptly. He again told me what happened in there was not to leave out of that room. "It's getting late. I think you should go home now. Here is a little something for you. I WILL SEE YOU THE NEXT TIME."

I said, "Okay," and then realized he had given me a crisp $100 bill. I asked what it was for.

He said, "It's plenty and much more for you. Keep your damn mouth closed and buy yourself something."

It was 11:00 p.m. when Jacob and I left. The valet brought the car, opened the car door for us and we left. As the stretch limo cruised down the street, you could only hear music. Jacob said nothing and neither did I.

Chapter 6
The Morning After

When I got home, the first thing I did was run and take a shower. Although there was no physical sexual activity between Reverend Smith and I, I still felt dirty. As I showered, I didn't think I could ever get clean enough. The thought of the smoke and all the alcohol was horrible. But what was really atrocious to me was the fact that Reverend Smith used his tongue to stimulate me. I had never experienced that before. That, I thought, was really gross.

As I bathed and prepared for bed, all kinds of thoughts ran through my head. I felt absolutely crazy. I tossed and turned throughout the night, wondering what in the world had just happened. I kept replaying the whole thing in my mind and I just couldn't believe what I had seen. I said to myself, "I know this has got to be a dream."

Before I knew it, my alarm clock was going off and it was time to get ready for church. "I wonder if I should just stay home today," I thought to myself. But that thought vanished as soon as it came because I knew that if I didn't go to church, Momma and Daddy would think something was wrong. After all, I was a faithful member of the church; I never missed a Sunday. I couldn't stand the thought of them asking me questions, and I certainly didn't want to give them room to do so.

So, the very next day, I found myself getting ready for church. I put on my Sunday "go-to-meeting clothes" and went on as if nothing had ever happened. What a mask I was wearing. On the outside, I looked like a normal teenage girl who was looking forward to a bright outlook on life. I had no kids, I had no bills, and I had no problems. All I had to do was get up and go to school every day so

I could make something out of myself. A bright future was right at my fingertips; all I had to do was reach out and grab it.

How, then, did I end up at a hotel the night before in the presence of a man that I was about to go and shout, "Hallelujah," every time he struck a good note on a song or every time he whooped when he preached?

I don't think my mind ever stopped asking questions from the time I left the hotel until the time I made it in to the sanctuary. The more I thought about it, the more I said to myself, "Whatever that was, it CAN NOT happen again. It just can't, Stacey. It just can't."

As the multitude of thoughts continued to run through my head, I finally had gotten myself dressed. Not realizing that my provocative style of dress, combined with my long hair and the beauty of my youth were perhaps part of my problem, I dressed just as I had dressed before. I wore sharp suits, and the style of the day was to wear your skirts short. I went just as I was. I was not concerned about what anybody thought about me or how I dressed. I loved Stacey and I made sure I looked good at all times.

If someone had a problem with the way I dressed; which I didn't care if they did or not; it was their problem, not mine. As far as I was concerned, there was no need to be concerned about what I wore. As long as I made it into the house of the Lord, I was just fine because I knew Jesus was not a respecter of persons. I knew that He knew it was what was in my heart that counted. It took me several years into my adulthood to realize how naïve I was. Hindsight is always 20/20 vision.

I took so much pride in riding in my own little car that I rarely rode to church with Momma and Daddy. Plus, this way worked out better just in case we wanted to go in different directions after church. I guess that's part of what helped contribute to my independence. By the time I made it to the church, I couldn't believe I had the courage to get up and face this man again. I wondered what would happen if I saw him up close. I wondered if he'd treat me any differently. I wondered if he'd give any indication at all of what had just happened last night.

As I got out of the car and made my way into the sanctuary, I wished I had a way to stop all the questions and thoughts from racing through my head. Needless to say, they kept right on coming. "Now Stacey, if he says something to you, you can't act like you're mad with him. Remember, he said what happened in the hotel room had to stay there. If you go in looking crazy, somebody will know something happened last night."

Now that this chapter of my life is long over, I can only wonder why I was beating myself over the head. I didn't put myself in that situation; he did. I just didn't have the sense enough to realize what was happening in the beginning.

The thoughts and questions continued. I was trying to figure out if what I thought happened really happened with the Pastor and me. Did I really go to a hotel on false beliefs? Is my momma going to find out? I was scared to death but I knew Pastor told me that no one was to know about last night. After saying my prayers and asking God to forgive me, I just felt like a nasty girl that was in the presence of all those men alone.

I was so disappointed in my pastor. What had happened the night before was the last thing I had expected. Could I tell my mother and she believe me? Could I tell a friend and they not make it a chain game and a longer story? "Girl, please," I thought to myself. "This is the evil deed that you're going to have to live with," are the words that stuck like glue in my head. I could only pray silently, "God, please have my back. I'm scared. Help me."

Once I made my way into the sanctuary and took a seat next to my parents, I realized I had never been so uncomfortable in my life. I asked myself, "Girl, how can you sit up here and look at this man?" As he opened his mouth to speak, all I could see in my head was a vision of all the gin, all the whiskey and the smoke-filled air that permeated the atmosphere of the plush hotel room. I felt ashamed that I had not confided in my parents. But how could I? They would have never believed me. After all, he was the minister that did their wedding ceremony. This was the pastor of the church. This man was married. Who would believe he made sexual advances to a young girl like me?

As the hundreds of questions soared through my head, I felt myself physically dazing as I again pondered over what had happened. "Stacey, pull yourself together, girl. You don't want Momma and Daddy asking you what's going on in your head while you're supposed to be worshiping the Lord. Come on now, Stacey. Shake it off. Shake it off, girl!"

Somehow, I snapped out of it, but as soon as I did, I found myself thinking all over again. Although, I was dressed up and sitting in a church amongst other fellow believers, I felt nasty. I felt dirty, like a dirty little girl. I tried to get into the service by clapping my hands to the music, by saying, "Amen" when it was appropriate, and by bowing my head during prayer. I went through the motions, but my heart was nowhere near God. It was just like the O'Jays sang in their song, "Your body's here with me but your mind is on the other side of town. **What if the man would have had sex with me? What if I had gotten raped by all of these "Men of the Cloth?"**

Unfortunately, the humiliation I felt would only continue because as time progressed and as the episodes continued, Reverend Smith told me I had to be in church everyday all day long, every Sunday. I couldn't believe it. What I experienced in that first episode would only escalate, and here this man was telling me I would have to face him every Sunday as if nothing had happened. What did he think I was? His play thing? Lord, have mercy!

The choir began to sing:

I woke up this mornin' with my mind
Stayed on Jesus.
Woke up this mornin' with my mind
Stayed on Jesus
Hallelu, Hallelu, Hallelujah!

As I sat going through the motions, the whole congregation joined the choir in singing. Without fail, a sister or brother, anybody would get happy and start shouting. Then one deacon would fall on his knees with the microphone in his hand, praying:

Lord, have mercy on us today.
Bless your people here today.
I'm down here on my knees;
Lord you sho been good to us all;
We could have been dead;
But you let us live another day.
Bless our pastor; the deacon board, the usher board, the choir; and
my family Lord.
Ha' mercy on us all Lord.
Bless me, your servant, Lord.
Bless the sick and the shut in;
Bless the bereaved families;
Bless the children
In the name of Jesus I pray, Amen.

The deacons would continue. They would read a scripture:

Open your Bibles to St. John Chapter 1:1-5 and it reads as follows:

1 In the beginning was the Word, and the Word was with God,
2 The same was in the beginning with God.
3 All things were made by him; and without him was not anything
   made that was made.
4 In him was life; and the life was the light of men
5 And the light shineth in darkness; and the darkness compre-
   hended it not.

Then, the reading deacon would say, "I have just read you verses
one through five of St. John, chapter one. Amen."

The service proceeded: I will now turn you over to the choir for an
A and B selection. The choir would come up and sing songs, one
upbeat song and one slow song.

The devotion, singing, collecting tithes and offering, everything
went on as usual. Then Pastor made his grand entrance. He was
dressed in a robe, wearing diamonds, a large gold bracelet, and a
gold chain. As if he were a king, he was escorted by two persons
into the pulpit. Watching this made me sick to my stomach. This
great big man came down with all of his charisma, singing one of

those good old time spirituals. At the same time, I couldn't help but observe all the innocent, heartbroken, hurting, needy people. They were emotional, crying and falling out over his singing and their needs. I was waiting to see if he could really function in the spiritual realm after I saw his last night's agenda.

This man could have won an Academy Award because after what I witnessed the night before, I was convinced that he had to be **a good actor.** There's no way he could have been sincere. There he was singing, praying, and preaching. People did their usual shouting, falling out and thinking he was some kind of king. How disgusting!

That Sunday I just had no feeling. I really did not want to be there but I was intimidated not to attend church and just too scared to say anything to anyone.

Chapter 7
My School Life

My senior year at Manual Arts High School was as much fun as it could be. I was alone. I missed being at home back in Louisiana with the people I knew. It was not the same. My high school there was big; but Manual Arts was too big. The students were much different in California than those in Louisiana. Where I grew up, everybody knew everybody but not here. I didn't mix with my peers. I stayed around my teachers and studied. Jaray and I used to eat lunch together. Some days, I would go to his classroom to watch him on the printing machine, which I found to be fascinating. I had never seen anything like it before. Jaray liked me, and I liked him a lot. He didn't talk much, but around him, I talked too much.

At that time, all I did was go to school and work. My goal was to get out of school quickly. My classes were so easy for me. I passed all of them with A's, B's and one C. We had a prom, but I decided not to go. Jaray had to work that night, and since I did not know anyone, I chose not to go. My biggest adventure was looking forward to graduating from high school. On graduation night, January 30, 1969, I was soooo happy.

My mother's expectations were high, so I had to go to college and get a degree. She and both of her sisters were teachers. My biological father's sister (Aunt Sicily) was a Teacher/Librarian, also. You may have surmised by now that not going to college was not an option for me. I received a four-year, fully paid scholarship to the University in Evanston, Illinois, in Speech and Drama. I did not want to go there or anywhere else away from home for that matter. (Remember, I also had scholarship offers to Spelman and Howard.) That meant leaving my momma and my new boyfriend. When I finished crying and carrying on, telling Momma that she was trying to get rid of me and that I didn't know anyone there, she decided to let me stay home. But she told me I was going to college. She was not kidding, and I knew that. She was very serious. Monday morning arrived, and she woke me up early to enroll at Compton Junior College (also known as Compton J.C.)

I had really good teachers my first semester. I took Psychology, English Grammar & Composition, P.E., Biology, Introduction to Sociology and Introduction to Music. Many people told me to stay away from the students' lounge because if you hung out there it could be 'contagious.' I went by a couple of times. People were playing card games, dominos, talking on the pay telephone, with plenty of socializing taking place. A light bulb flashed in my head that warned, "Oh no, stay out of there. Stay focused. You have a goal to achieve. You can not do it being in the lounge." I heeded the warning and stayed away.

I applied for and got a teacher's aide job with Los Angeles Unified School District. I worked at Markham Junior High several days a week after I left the junior college, and I also worked at Sears (at Vermont & Slauson) part time. After one semester at Compton J.C., I enrolled in Pepperdine College in Los Angeles, August 1970. At that time I was steadily dating my boyfriend, Jaray, who attended Compton J.C., and who also worked in Burbank in the evening. When I was enrolled in Pepperdine, the college situation was different from what I was used to. This school was private, expensive, and predominately Caucasian. Momma signed for me to get a student loan.

My classes were geared towards Speech and Drama because I was still set on a major in acting. I attended the first trimester, which was a truly rude awakening in so many ways. The instructors were very different, although I had some very good ones. Chapel attendance several days a week was mandatory, as were Religion classes.

Even though I did well at Compton Junior College, I received one fail, two D's, and one C my first trimester at Pepperdine. I was embarrassed and humiliated. I knew my momma was going to lay hands on me for sure when she found out about my grades, so I did not tell her. Instead, I eloped and left home. Yes, I did. I married Jaray. My older brother, Sam, Jr. helped me do the dirty work. We got married at a wedding chapel on Vermont Avenue called Bride's Choice Wedding Chapel.

Momma was so hurt she did not know what to do. She cried so much I thought she was going to be hospitalized. I pretended that I did not care. I cared and I was scared. She did not yet have my grades. The worst was yet to come.

For our honeymoon, Jaray took a vacation, and we went to Louisiana to meet his mother for Christmas. By the time we returned from Louisiana, my grades had arrived. I was forced to listen to Momma's sermon about me going to school. She did not care if I was married or not, I was going to get an education. Jaray also informed me he was not planning on having a dumb wife. "Okay," I thought, "that was it." I did not die. I was yelled at, but I survived it. Now it was time for me to buckle down. When I signed up for my classes at Pepperdine, I also received a letter that I was on academic probation. I continued to take classes at both schools and work. The next trimester, I earned four A's and one B. That still didn't make my grade point average strong enough to take me off probation. I stayed on it for three trimesters, which is equivalent to one year. That motivated me to study, study and study some more.

I pledge in a sorority at Pepperdine called KKK (Kappa Kappa Kappa). It was fun. I had to do all of my initiation on campus. I stayed away from home (on campus) a few days. I was so glad I did not have to live on campus. That experience was really not for me.

I kept in touch with my counselors from both schools in order to see what courses I needed for graduation from each school. I was so happy in February 1972, when I earned an A.A. degree from Compton Junior College, and August 1972, when I earned a Bachelor's degree from Pepperdine College.

Chapter 8
My First Marriage

On December 14, 1970, I eloped with the first love I had in Los Angeles, California. I was 18-years-old and Jaray was 20. He was a handsome, six-foot, brown-skinned, strong Black man. We were married for 12 years. He was my high school sweetheart and a neat freak; everything had to be in order. He kept the lawn beautiful. He maintained the cars. He used to drink and tell me that nice ladies stay at home while men went out on the town. Yes, we were married for 12 years; however, the longevity in a marriage is no signal for a happy marriage. I had 12 years of being mentally and physically abused. He pulled a gun on me on three separate occasions, and thank God, I am still alive to tell about it.

During our 12 years of marriage, we were separated three times. With each separation, I found myself back with Pastor Smith. After the birth of our third child, I told God that if he let me get away this time I would not look back. My baby Mark was only two-weeks-old when I left him for the last time.

We got a one-bedroom apartment in Compton. Jaray had his car, and I had mine. We were both working, and I was going to school. My aspirations were to finish school and become an actress. My older brother liked Jaray; they became friends. My now deceased brother Sam, Jr., had a celebration for us. He knew a gentleman who lived near Pepperdine, and this man allowed us to have a small celebration at his house. Sam, Jr. had a very sweet personality; to know him was to love him. He was mischievous, but at the same time, he had a heart of gold. I loved my brother.

After I got married, I still did not know how to cook, wash, iron, or sew. When I cooked breakfast the day after our marriage, I burned both the bacon and the eggs. Jaray sweetly said that it was very good. Everything was either undercooked or overcooked. One day he decided to teach me the basics of cooking.

When Jaray got his vacation during the month of December, we drove to Baton Rouge, Louisiana. It was the honeymoon/vacation from hell. My biological father lived only two blocks from Jaray's mother. When we arrived, my husband got a very warm reception from his family. I got a breath of coldness that I was not anticipating from his mother, sister, and brothers. I was disappointed. I went to see my daddy (Sam, Sr.), the peanut man, who lived three streets away. He had been selling peanuts since the age of 12 or 13; he is now 86-years-old. He always had a very loud voice. I was very fearful of the tone of his voice. He told me I should not have gotten married so soon, then he asked me why I rushed to do so. He stated, "You don't know anything about the family you've married off into, but since you have gotten married, try to make the best of it."

I also went to see my paternal grandmother, the late Ma Bonnie. She did not talk much. She was a very neat lady, one who kept her kitchen spotless. I enjoyed watching her. She took so much pride in all she did. She even ironed her sheets and tablecloths. While I was there, she washed my clothes and cooked for me.

I traveled to visit my maternal great-great-aunt in Opelousas named Elaine. She loved me so much; she always thought I was an angel. She bought my first piano and taught me how to pray on my knees. When I was living in Louisiana, I would go to New Orleans every year and stay with her. She was a good old Southern Christian. She had an old fashioned record player and used to play Mahalia Jackson songs. Every Wednesday night, the two of us would have our prayer meeting, where she would sing songs, read the Bible, and pray. She wished Jaray and I well in our marriage and told us that if we did not have a disagreement we would be living a lie. She explained, "No two people can live under the same roof all the time and agree to everything all the time." Aunt Elaine and her husband Uncle Frank were married 51 years, then he passed away. After that she moved to Opelousas, where she had been born and owned property.

Aunt Elaine told us we needed to pray, and pray without ceasing. She also informed me that she was going to give me a down payment on a home. She believed that since we were married, Jaray and I should have a home. "If you have children, they should be brought up in a home, with a yard and plenty of space," was her philosophy.

Jaray stayed with his relatives during the time, and I stayed with mine. That was not a very good start for our marriage. When it was time for us to leave, we said our good-byes and left. On the way home, he remained silent. When we arrived, my goal was to locate the right home for us to purchase. Mr. Bill Bagby, a very nice man who had no hands, helped us to find a lovely, three-bedroom home with a fireplace in Compton. Aunt Elaine sent me the money, as she promised, then we moved.

Momma gave us furniture to help us get started, and I continued my schooling and working. Then my mother-in-law started calling collect, asking my husband for money to help her pay her bills. It would have been okay with me, but I minded the person-to-person collect calls to him. Previously, he admonished me that his money was his and my money was ours. Whenever his mother or any of his relatives called collect Jaray ordered me to accept the calls. That was not a very good feeling. I ended up working for us, and he was working for his family and himself. This went on almost every month. He took my checks and gave me an allowance.

Jaray had a younger brother that got into mischief quite a bit. When his mother called, wanting this brother to come live with us, I refused. This is when Jaray began abusing me. He screamed at me, and I screamed at him. My aunt had not helped us buy a house in order to fill it with his siblings or my in-laws. He slapped me so hard I saw stars and stripes. He was six feet and weighed 180 pounds; I was 5' 2" and weighed 90-95 pounds. There was no need to try to fight him; I would have been fighting a losing battle. Problems had begun. I was told once your spouse hits you, it becomes easier and easier the next time. Jaray told me he would never strike me again. I continued my school. When the telephone bill arrived every month, the weekly, no secret collect phone calls appeared.

Summer came along with two of Jaray's siblings. One stayed with us, sporting an attitude. The other one stayed with her in-laws. I tried to do everything to make my sister-in-law happy, but she had been programmed too well to change her behavior. For seven days, our home was filled with tension. But I got over that. My husband and I did not speak for three to four weeks. Whenever I would attempt to talk to him, he would get up and walk right past me, as if I did not exist.

One day during my last trimester in school, his family called. His brother had shot his little sister in the head. I told him to take our credit card and purchase a ticket to fly home. The family called collect almost every hour. The boy took the three-year-old to the hospital in a bicycle's basket. No one knew where the mother was at the time of the accident. The three-year-old child died. I told him as soon as I completed my exams, I would meet him there, even if my in-laws did not want me around. I went to support my husband. When I arrived, I was treated as if I did something wrong. Jaray would leave me at the house while he and his mother did errands. His siblings had all planned to dress alike at the funeral and they did. I was left completely out of the picture. The day of the funeral, I was not allowed to sit with my husband. Instead, I was relegated to sitting all the way in the back of the church.

When I returned home, I continued my goal to finish school. During this time, we tried to conceive, but were unsuccessful. I spoke to Jaray about adopting a baby, but he adamantly refused. Because I would not let siblings come live in our house, so he was not about to adopt someone else's child to bring into our house.

I thank Jesus, because in August 1972, I graduated from Pepperdine. I was overjoyed. Immediately I began searching for a better job. I took the probation officers' written test, where I scored 95/100. Unfortunately, I did not get the job. I did the required student teaching, one semester at Bret Harte Junior High and a semester a Gardena High School. I had a job interview at Jordan High School. The interview went fine, but as I left the school, a male student approached me. Thinking I was a student also, he asked, "What's up, baby?" I was 20-years old, and these kids were

15-to 18- years old. Teaching high school was not on my agenda at that time. I drove around the city, spotted a really nice looking school on 69th and Broadway. I stopped and inquired if I could speak with the principal. Even though I had no appointment scheduled with her, she agreed to see me. Guess what? She hired me. I was 20, excited, and thanked Jesus for leading me to this opportunity.

Chapter 9
My First Teaching Assignment

The day was January 29, 1973; Mrs. Deena Brown had hired me to teach Special Ed transitional students at Mary McLeod Bethune Junior High School. I was so happy and excited. My beginning salary was a whopping $800 a month. This was so nice. I had a real job, working with children. Mrs. Brown was a very smart and very strict lady. I was hired as a long-term substitute. In order to become a probationary teacher, I had to take the required test. During the course of the first semester I took and passed the test.

Mrs. Brown would often come in my classroom unannounced and observe me. She carried her notebook and pen. She would nod her head as if to say, "Continue," while I taught. At the end of the workday, I went to her office for the evaluation. I was so scared when I went in there that I was shaking in my shoes and sweating in my palms. She always told me I was doing a fine job. Mrs. Brown was always so quiet and professional. She reminded me of a strict momma.

I left home at 6 a.m. to get to work early, but I always stopped at my momma's house first. We would have coffee and hot chocolate together every morning. Then I arrived at school between 7:00-7:15, read my Bible, ate breakfast and prepared for my students. On Saturdays, I cleaned my house and went shopping.

My husband went out every Friday night, but refused to take me with him because 'nice ladies stay home.' Only men hang out. He had double standards. He would not take me out to dinner unless it was an anniversary or birthday. He said it was better to eat at home. On Sundays, I would attend church alone. Soon I found a lady minister who pastored a small church and began attending there. I started going to the Friday night services, which lasted 4-5 hours.

Jaray did not believe I was attending church. He followed me a few times, although I was not aware of it. I invited him to church services, and one night, out of curiosity, he came. The evangelist was also a prophetess. She had Jaray stand and told him he had plans to leave his wife. She proceeded to tell him that he would be like a fish on dry land, struggling to get water. Afterwards, he sat down. This evangelist spoke to people in a manner that only that person understood what she was talking about. That particular night, she told me she saw me rocking my own little baby. I laughed because the doctors had told me I was not going to have any children.

I was so in love with children I would occasionally bring them home with me from school. I had one little girl named Yvonne, who thought I was her momma. She even called me momma. Yvonne would come to my house at least three times a week and every weekend. She was at my house when a long distance call came from Jaray's sister. Jaray was on the telephone unaware that Yvonne was eavesdropping. Jaray's sister told him that he could not tell anyone what she was about to say, and that the brother who shot their little sister had raped both her children.

Yvonne then asked me to take her to McDonald's so I did. She told me about the conversation, then begged me not to say anything. I did not say anything while she was there.

Jaray had his own way of doing things. The following week, he asked if his brother could come and live with us. I refused and told him he did not even know his brother because they had never really lived together. I got beat up again. Jaray gave me a black eye. One of my friends in the teachers' lounge asked me if I ran into a doorknob. I responded that I ran into my husband's fist. Then, I went into my classroom feeling all depressed. After that, there was a silent treatment for a few weeks at home.

The summer came and in July I flew to Louisiana with my now deceased stepfather. He stayed in a hotel, while I stayed with my biological father and Ma Bonnie. I did not visit my in-laws at all. The two of us stayed about ten days. My uncle, who was a minister, and my stepfather were very close. My stepfather would go fishing with some of my uncle's friends, then bring the catch home, clean them, and eat fried fish at my uncle's house.

In the early 1970's, my late uncle would allow me to speak at his church, Star Hill Missionary Baptist Church, in Baton Rouge, Louisiana. The trip and all the good food I knew I would be eating excited me. Good gumbo, dirty rice, barbeque, boudin, pigs' feet, ham hocks, greens, chitterlings, rice, hog cracklings, and hog head cheese, etc. Well most of the time when I flew, God would reveal things to me; he revealed a message to me on that flight. This particular year, I was so happy thinking about all the good food waiting for me and how I was going to pig out. But, contrary to my thoughts, God directed me to be on a seven-day fast, drinking water only. "Oh, man, why?" I thought. But I obeyed. My folks could not believe I was not eating as much as I like to eat.

That Sunday when I got to church, the anointing was so heavy; people started falling out as soon as God had me open my mouth. I do not profess to be a soloist, but as the words of the song "Only Believe" came from my mouth, the presence of the Lord was there. People were being healed, saved and delivered. I praise God for my uncle, the late, great Rev. Herbert Gray. The Lord blessed the people that day through words of inspiration. It was truly a blessing.

In August 1973 when we left Louisiana and got back home, I discovered I was three months pregnant with my first child. Jaray and I were happy. I was going back to my teaching job, and we were expecting our first baby in February. My principal assigned me to be the Drama teacher/coordinator. I put together a Thanksgiving production and also a Christmas production. They were very successful. I worked until the end of the semester, but did not return after it.

Chapter 10
My First Child

O n February 24, 1974, I gave birth to a beautiful, healthy, eight-pound baby girl. My mother and my husband were there with me the whole time I was in labor. She was born very early on a sunny Sunday morning. I thought she was never going to get here. I stayed in labor for 16 hours. Jaray and I went through our little selfish disagreement. He wanted to name her after his late sister Cheryl Ann, but I refused. Jaray and I finally came to an agreement and named her Marilyn.

When I got home, I was so pleased that the pregnancy was over. Jaray was such a proud and happy father. He held the baby. She was born at Kaiser Hospital. We had rooming-in service. I could pull the special drawer out and my baby girl would be in the room with me; if I pushed the drawer back in she would be in the nursery. This gave us time to learn how to feed, bathe, and spoil her. Both of my brothers came to the hospital. They were very proud uncles and both wanted to be Godparents, so I allowed it. Marilyn had three sets of godparents.

I went through some bad postpartum blues. I was so depressed and did not want to eat. I remember my mother coming over, hand-feeding me. But I loved my brand new, live baby doll and thanked God for giving me this wonderful bundle of joy. She was given so many gifts.

My maternal grandmother, Mary, came over. She prayed for us and told me I was not leaving my house for six weeks. Then she held the baby. Grandma told me that the Lord had blessed us with a healthy baby, and we needed to live and take care of her. I stayed home until the next semester began.

Grandma kept my baby girl while I was at work. I would get up extra early to stop at Momma's house, take the baby to my grandmother, and then go to work. I paid $25 a week for childcare. I did not like the idea of leaving my little princess, but I had to go to work. When I started work again, I was very happy to be receiving a full check once more. At that time, I was still allowing Jaray to take my checks. On Saturdays, I took my baby to the Cerritos Mall. On Sundays, we attended church. In fact, after my baby's first checkup, her next stop was church. Proverbs 22:6 says, "Train up a child in the way he should go, and when he is old he will not depart from it."

My husband did not attend church with us. When we got home from church, his friends were sitting at the dining room table, playing dominos and drinking alcohol. He expected me to fix dinner and feed everyone. I did for a while, but I felt like I was being treated like a maid. He did not appreciate me, and his friends disrespected me. After they had been drinking my husband would go to the bathroom or somewhere else in the house. Then his friends would always say inappropriate things to me. I complained to my husband about it, but he never believed me. I would get my baby's things ready for the next week and get myself ready for work. If Jaray drank too much, we would argue, and I occasionally got hit. After I decided to keep my money, Jaray became very angry. He beat me, so I ran off with my little girl who was 17-months old. We lived in an apartment in the country club.

During the marriage, Pastor and I were still communicating. Occasionally, I would go out and meet him. I was scared as hell but I took the chances. All he had to say was when and I did. When I told him I moved out, he wanted to make sure I was okay. He told me he was leaving a package with the secretary for me. When I got the package, I was shocked. It was an envelope with cash only. I was shocked but happy. I made a telephone call to say thank you.

I got lonely for Jaray and visa versa. We called each other and while I was talking to him, the sounds of "**After all that we been through, Do you still Love Me" could be heard in the background.** Anyway, we went on a couple of, "Can we get back together" dates and it happened.

After about three months in the new apartment, Marilyn and I moved back home. We got along for a while and then hell broke loose again.

Chapter 11
The Birth of Jaray, Jr.

In 1977, my pretty little princess, Marilyn, told me she wanted a sister or brother. Jaray and I felt like she needed a playmate also. In September of that year, I enrolled in Azusa Pacific College to work on my Master's degree in Educational Psychology. Amazingly, when school began, I was expecting our second baby. I was not discouraged with returning to school. Like David who encouraged himself in the book of Samuel from the Bible, I prayed and encouraged myself, too. Jaray was against me going back to school. I had arguments and physical fights with him. He both physically and mentally abused me. This is known as domestic violence today. He told me I had enough education. "Forget him," I thought. "I am going to school to better myself. I want more than a B.A. I really want a Ph. D. God, help me one step at a time, and help me live my dream. Pregnancy is not about to put a halt on me," were the thoughts that resonated in my mind.

Jaray would go out and come home angry, cursing me. I was feisty and did not keep my mouth closed when he said something idiotic to me. I was not the "okay, honey" wife. I had to say what was on my mind. I know and believed in a man far greater than Jaray, who we call Jesus. I felt too blessed to be stressed. This motivated me to really want to do something with my life.

While I was attending Azusa Pacific, working on my degree, I was also teaching at Bethune Junior High and taking care of our daughter. We had clusters at Azusa at the time I was attending. I thought our cluster was the best. I had classmates from Compton Unified, L.A. Unified, Pomona Unified, and Cerritos Unified. We really bonded and got along very well.

I had a goal. My baby was on the way. I read, studied, taught school and was beaten by Jaray. I did all my class work, took my tests, sent my daughter to preschool, attended church, and prayed that my unborn baby would be intelligent and healthy.

I took the written exam and passed it; next, I was on a team for my oral exam and passed it. The panel team informed me I had passed and did not need to answer any more questions.

My Marilyn was excited about her momma giving her a little brother or sister. Although she was only four-years old, I know she had to have heard the arguments and fights between her daddy and me. I had a very dear friend, Ann, attending Azusa with me, who I confided in. She would listen to me and try to console me on those days I attended school crying. My face was swollen and I was feeling really hurt. She was a happily married woman. I used to listen to her talk about life, her children, and her husband.

After taking my oral exam, I was eagerly looking forward to marching with my graduation class on May 6, 1978. I stayed on the honor roll the entire time and graduated with honors, but I could not march with the class that day because God had decided to make this day a most memorable day in my life, a day that will never be forgotten. That day, my second child, a son, Jaray, Jr. was born.

Chapter 12

Separation

Everyday Marilyn would ask to hold her Jaray, Jr. She loved him so much. I would allow her to hold him in my presence. A few days later, I left him in the bed and left her in the room with him. When I returned to the room, he was not there. I asked Marilyn if she knew where her brother had gone. She said, "No." I looked throughout the house, calling to a baby only a few weeks old. She walked beside me calling him also. Finally, she went into the living room and told me where he was. She had placed him in the fireplace. We talked about it. I told her neither she nor Jaray, Jr. should ever be placed in the fireplace. She said, "Okay, Mommy."

Life was really different now with two children. I was a very happy mother. Jaray, Jr. was my Mother's Day gift. I took Marilyn to preschool and Jaray, Jr. to my maternal grandmother's house. She lived very close to the school where I was working. Seatbelts and a car seat were not as important back then. I would nurse Jaray, Jr. on the way to my grandmother's house and go to her house at lunchtime. Grandma Mary would always tell me what a good baby he was.

The four of us celebrated Thanksgiving together and were very happy. But by the time Jaray, Jr. was seven-months old, Jaray and I had separated again. I've always liked nice, small cars and wanted one. Jaray wanted a big car. We bought a 1979 Coupe de Ville cream-yellow Cadillac that was deducted from my check every month at the credit union. He told me to drive the car to work and he would use it on the weekends. Our other car was a BMW. Jaray, Sr. kept them clean, oil checked, and gassed up every week.

After we ate our Thanksgiving dinner together at home, the two children and I went to my grandmother's house to eat. We often ate at Grandma's house. Jaray, Sr. would never accompany us. I took pictures of Jaray, Jr.'s first Thanksgiving with a big drumstick. He was walking around in the baby walker. I tried to see if he would walk alone but he did not. I remember giving Marilyn her first drumstick and she promptly took off walking by her self, taking giant steps. I took lots of pictures.

The day after Thanksgiving I did my Christmas shopping; I always get up early in the morning to go shopping. December 24, 1978, my late uncle, a very prominent minister in Baton Rouge, was on his way to California to be with all of us for Christmas. We always had a good time praying together, eating together, and being merry. I was excited. I got my two children dressed and ready to go to Grandma's house.

However, to my surprise, Jaray, Sr. told me the car was not leaving the house that day. Being 26-years old, (**GROWN**) working everyday, a mother of two children, I knew he had to be kidding. I wondered, "Who is he talking to? Where are these jokes coming from?" As I attempted to walk out the door, he grabbed Marilyn and pushed her in the bedroom, then he grabbed Jaray, Jr. and threw him across the room, and finally he grabbed my hair, threw me on the floor, and beat my head as if it were a basketball. Again, I was physically abused. This time Jaray, Jr. and I were taken to Kaiser Hospital. Jaray had broken my thumb and given me a concussion. Fighting him was impossible. The two babies were hysterical. I still left with my children, but I was beaten up. It was Christmas time; the happiest time of the year for me. I had purchased the children toys and other family members gifts. I ended up being escorted by the Compton Police to my home (that my great-great aunt helped us buy for a wedding gift) to get my Christmas gifts. While I gathered the gifts, Jaray called me many derogatory names. I am so grateful that the domestic laws have changed for the better and are now really enforced. At that time, I felt like I was not being properly protected.

My parents were furious over this incident. I was forced to allow this cowardly man who beat me to remain in our house because it was in both of our names. My children did not deserve to experience this kind of abuse. My babies were innocent. Why were they experiencing this? The children and I stayed with my mother and my late stepfather. I pretended to be happy, especially for Jaray, Jr.; it was his first Christmas. We had Christmas dinner at my late grandmother's house with the entire family. I had a bruised face and my head felt like a large thumping ball.

I knew I needed my own space and independence. I felt crushed. My mother and stepdad did not mind us living there. My daughter attended school where my mother taught, and my grandmother kept Jaray, Jr. I got a restraining order placed on Jaray and I stated that I was never going back to him. Soon, I left Marilyn with my mom and stepdad. Jaray, Jr. stayed with my grandmother, and I lived in the Mustang Motel on Western Avenue along with going back to being a mistress/madam.

Jaray, Jr. was such a good baby. My grandmother said instead of him crawling to where he wanted to go, he would roll there. If Jaray, Jr. was put in one place, he would stay right there until told to do something different. I missed being present to observe all these precious little moments. I was very uncomfortable and did not feel right. I prayed that God would help me find a place for my children and me to be together under the same roof. I was a woman of faith then and still am. Jesus said in the Bible, "And all things whatsoever ye shall ask in prayer, believing, ye shall receive" (Matthew 21:22).

I prayed and believed, I had faith, and I received a new home for my children and me on May 25, 1979. My friend, Della, who was in real estate, helped me find the home. It belonged to a divorcing couple who wanted out of the house. It had three bedrooms and two bathrooms. I thought it was perfect. And it was perfect. They wanted a large sum of money down to assume the loan. Praise God for my church and my mother. I knew that being a faithful tither I could go to my father's storehouse. (Believe me, readers, the biblical principle of tithing works.) From both of them, I got an interest-free loan. What a mighty God I serve.

The three of us moved into our home and were very happy. My children did not deserve to be in a parental-abusive situation. God reminds me in His Word that He will supply my needs according to His riches in glory. And my children and I needed a home. Jaray, Jr. was one year old. We had no furniture, but praise God; we had a roof over our heads. That Memorial Day weekend, we went out and purchased a stove, refrigerator, and a bed for Jaray, Jr. and Marilyn. We bought groceries; everything felt good. Thank God for Jesus. My pastor came over to bless our home. All I could say was what Jesus once said, "Father, I thank thee that thou hast heard me" (John 11:41).

Jr. was still in diapers. We had a brown dog, a boxer, named 'Mike'. Jaray, Jr. loved Mike. As a matter of fact, he loved all animals; he would go out in the big backyard with the dog. Mike would pull his diaper off, and then Jaray, Jr. would bite the dog. They had fun together. We had a live in nanny, who kept Jaray, Jr. very nice and clean. She changed his clothes at least three times and day and kept the house immaculate. She stayed with us from Sunday night to Friday evening. The kids and I ate out every Friday night. In the summer, we did little things like picnics in the backyard. I had the outside of the house painted that summer, and just enjoyed being home.

Because I was so embarrassed that my co-workers knew of my marital difficulties, I put in for a transfer and changed schools. It's called survival. I started working in Canoga Park when I discovered Jaray, Jr. had chronic asthma and a lot of allergies. For a long time he did not talk. Doctors told me he would be retarded. When he cried, his mouth twisted. The doctors stated that it was from dead nerve cells. He just pointed at everything he wanted because he would not or could not talk. I took him to many doctors. Then I heard about acupuncture. I took him for treatment, too. The combination helped him to talk. I thank God for two healthy children.

Chapter 13
Caught Up

Regardless of how humiliated I felt the first Sunday after that fateful night, my phone calls from Jacob continued. Before I knew it, going to various hotels to meet Pastor Smith became second nature. After awhile, he was bold enough to call me himself. I had gotten my own private telephone. I was working part-time at Sears and Mom and Dad thought I was paying my telephone bill with my own money. I continued to be apprehensive in the beginning, but the bait that I was receiving began to look awfully good. The telephone was only one perk. The love **of money is the root of all evil. (1Timothy 6:10)**.

Other magnets included the fact that we would always meet at the finest of hotels. I'd eat the best food, whatever I wanted, and I always left with plenty of money. The first $100 bill I received was nothing compared to what I would receive later on down the line. As time went on, I earned what I thought was a place of prestige. When Pastor would travel out of town, I could always expect a ticket to meet him at one of the finest hotels in the city. Not only would I give him sex, but if he had Pastor-friends there, I was made available to them as well. I knew in my heart that I was raised much better and had no reason to do what I found myself doing. As a 17-year-old girl, I just didn't have the fortitude to walk away. I was simply caught up. Never would I want my daughters or any one else's daughter to live such a life.

One Saturday evening at around 6:00, I found myself driving up to one of the hotels for another episode. I would leave my car with the valet attendants, which is what I was instructed to do. I did as I was told. My next directive was to call and get connected to Pastor Smith's room. I did. He asked me where I was and I told him

I was in the lobby. He proceeded to give me the room number and I would get on the elevator and go up.

Approaching the room, I could hear the music playing, "This is what I do to get you in the mood. Baby, this is what I do to get you in the mood. We can take a shower....I do it just for you baby." (It was an old Whispers song.) Wasn't this a trip? Here was the Pastor singing the Whispers' songs. He had such a beautiful voice, and to hear him sing anything just blew my young stupid mind.

As other music played, we would two-step, and we were just as high as we wanted to be. The alcohol had given us a buzz that was out of this world. This giant of a man was very light on his feet. If I didn't see it for myself, I would probably have a hard time believing it because he was over 200 pounds, 6'5". Yet, he could dance and he kept up with me when we danced together. We would dance till we just could not dance anymore.

This was such a big man, he nicknamed himself "Poor Ti**y." Whenever he would see me on our rendezvous, he would greet me with, "Here is my baby with the biting p*s*y." I would just smile and blush, "What does that mean?"

"Come over here and let me touch it," would be his response.

I would walk over and he would ask me, "Did you buy some sexy bloomers?"

We both would laugh, but deep down inside, I was so embarrassed and ashamed. My heart would be pounding, "Lord, help me."

I would try to talk about religion and he would answer a few questions but got right back to foolish talk. He'd say things like, "The Bible says the only woman that was a virgin was Mary."

Again, I would ask, "Okay. What does that mean?"

He would close his eyes and smile showing his big dimple and grab my big breasts and squeeze them one at the time. Then he would grab both of them and start unbuttoning my top awkwardly and start sucking on them. I was shy. I had the perfect breasts and I really felt he felt that way also. I think I wore maybe a 36 C cup, which means he enjoyed every minute of his foreplay.

Sitting in the chair he would tell me, "Grab my John and rub it up and down. Caress it and squeeze it until it is what you want it to be." My heart would be beating so fast I knew it had to show in my appearance. "Angela (alter ego) aren't you relaxed? I promise I will not bite you. I'm only gonna eat you up and lick you up and down," he said as if that was just fine.

I drank glass after glass of white zinfandel, trying to not imagine what was about to happen. He was so drunk. Not only was he sweating like a bull but the more he drank, the more slouchy and wild he got. He snorted more cocaine. He took his tongue and licked me all over my face and neck. He began to suck on my breast, and next in my navel. I was getting hot. My vagina started thumping and thumping. "Oh God, what is this man doing to me?" I was wet in my panties. I was hot as a blazing fire.

The next thing I remembered was being on top of this big gigantic man riding him. I felt like I was on a big boat riding the waves in water. He was huffing and puffing. His eyes were closed and he was all into it. He would scream out, "Who am I?"

The magic words were," Big Daddy! You are the best!"

After my pony ride, I would pass completely out. My head was spinning like I had ridden a roller coaster. Eventually, I threw up the liquor I could not handle. When I awakened the next morning, cash money was left on the nightstand and he was gone. He left no written words, only cash. I got up with a banging headache, showered and then went home.

On another occasion, one of his minister friends came to do a revival. He had a physical handicap and I was afraid of him. I begged Reverend Smith not to make me sleep with him. He told me to take some drinks and do whatever I had to do. He told me not to be afraid. "He wants you badly," he said. As it got later into the night all the other ministers and Reverend Smith were in their de ja vu. This afflicted old man asked me if we could excuse ourselves from the room. "I would like you to join me in my elaborate room," he said. I took a whole bottle of gin and gulped it down in two or three shots. I really did not want to remember this night at all. Just imagine this man taking his clothes off and trying to be sexy. It was so disgusting that after the sexual encounter, I regurgitated all over him and me.

There were many episodes with me and Reverend Smith. We probably went to nearly all of the nice hotels on Century Boulevard going toward the airport. We cannot exclude the Hilton downtown, the Bonaventure, The Olympian in Mid Town Los Angeles, The Airport Park Hotel next to The Forum and the Hilton Long Beach.

During the course of all my escapades with Reverend Smith and his posse, I was able to travel to different cities as he preached revivals. He would fly me in and we would have breakfast in the hotel and lunch out on the town. It didn't matter where we were. After our time out on the town, we would come back to the hotel to rest up for the night so we'd be ready for church.

We would dance and party after revival. I had the opportunity to bring some other women as time went on and I guess he trusted me to do this. He suggested that I bring some other females that would like to have fun but he warned me that they were going to have to, "Keep their damn mouths shut." I eventually talked it up with some of my associates. One of my associates, Jean, slept with a Pastor from Shreveport, Louisiana. This foolish man gave her his church address and home address. He promised to financially care for her. What was most amazing about this Pastor was that not only did he and Jean freak, drink and have sex, but he also took nude pictures with her.

Jean was a single woman with three children. According to her, she had nothing to lose. When he did not fulfill his financial obligations that he promised, Jean wasted no time in sending the nude pictures to the righteous reverend's house. Reverend Kanord would constantly refer to Los Angeles as the sin city and his wife was very adamant about him visiting without her. Needless to say, he and his wife divorced after the package came in the mail.

Jean was my girl, but my friend Rene that lived two blocks from me was really my road dog. On most of our escapades, she was right there with me. She made me overcome a lot of things I feared when it came to entering the hotels. We would talk about how much longer I had to do this without getting caught. She never encouraged me, but she never discouraged me either. She was one to go along with the program. Until this very day I have never seen her angry. She had a lovely smile and she was a very easy person to get along with. Whoever Reverend Smith set her up with, she had no complaints. These women came to freak with his Associate Pastors that were well known in California: Los Angeles, Compton and Oakland; Atlanta; Shreveport, New Orleans, Dallas, and Chicago. Some of them are prominent Pastors to this very day

A couple of years had gone by and I had gotten very deep into this lifestyle. Although I had separated from Jaray, I still was hanging out. I guess this was due, in part, to the fact that Jaray was one hell of a man to live with. He was mean, always saying evil things to me, and I couldn't trust him. (**He tried to make me have a low self–esteem**). Big Daddy told me I had no business getting married anyway. He felt like since he was taking care of me, I had no reason to tell my husband about him, and I didn't. Now that I'm older and more mature, I can now ask, "What kind of attitude was that for one who was supposed to instill the values and sanctity of marriage in others?"

Big Daddy told me he still expected me to have my visits with him even if I decided to return to Jaray again. Yes, he insisted that committing adultery was okay. Unfortunately, I accepted his view on the matter. When there were church outings, my ticket was paid for and I was expected to be at my designated location and act accordingly. This was first very awkward. He made sure I was not too far from him and his wife's table. Any extra that I needed, I got it that evening. Of course, this lady was very beautiful and she was the first lady. "How could he being doing this to us," I wondered.

Later into escapades with him, I eventually saw other women from the church going up the elevator while I was coming down or vice versa. Nothing really clicked into my stupid innocent head that it was no accident these women were here at the same hotel and that they belonged to the same church as me and Big Daddy. How dumb could one be?

Sometimes I would be shocked to see all the pastors that were in "the circle." Most of them had a theme name to their church or title. I would say, "Oh, and you are Reverend _____." (I would say the church's theme. If I were to say it here, you'd know exactly who I am talking about. Remember, that's not the objective of this book.) They would stare at Reverend Smith and he would tell them, "She knows not to talk. Don't worry, all her buddies are not going to call your name." He mentioned Jean could not come back anymore because of what she did to Reverend Kanord.

Whenever we were in Oakland, we would go to the pier for lunch. Pastor Smith and his friends were well dressed. They wore the sharpest suits, ties and shoes. They were always sharp from head to toe. As we were sitting eating, one of Big Daddy's friends said, "Doc, she a pretty young thing," and smiled.

Pastor Smith said, "I know, man, but she is trying to get away from me. The news is out."

I looked at him with a surprised look and asked, "What are you talking about?"

Reverend Smith told me, "Don't play with my emotions. I will hurt you real bad." I did not even reply. He continued, "I had to get her away from Los Angeles to let her enjoy San Francisco."

Seeing my loss of interest in the conversation, he asked, "Why aren't you smiling with that pretty dimple?"

I timidly looked up and smiled, blinking my eyes flirtatiously. Most of the time I was embarrassed and ashamed of this life I was living but it would often come to my mind that there was no one on the face of the earth who would believe me. The women that were going with me were all for the "game." They enjoyed the money and the private parties.

One night after Pastor Smith had preached a service at the church, he asked me who the girl with me was. I told him she was my cousin. He insisted that I bring her to the hotel. I told him I could not promise and that she was not a talker. Nonetheless, it happened. After church services, we rode to the Olympian Hotel in mid Los Angeles. Nancy, Rene and I went through my routine of going through the valet parking. We made our way to the room and knocked on the door. Before Nancy walked in the door good, these men of the cloth were so drunk; they were all over her like dogs in heat. Their shirts were hanging out of their pants, their ties were off and some of them had their shoes off. The two that attacked her at the door broke the buttons off of her blouse and were licking her face. Her bra ended up broken and she said, "Damn!"

I thought she was going to holler, "Rape," but she said, "Can I have a drink first?" She drank about three straight small glasses of whiskey and hit the joint twice. (Yes, marijuana was part of the game as well.) She started relaxing and two of them were just all on top of her in front of all of us.

While this was going on, I was dancing with Reverend Marvin Hale. I was wiggling my bouncing behind while his old ass was hitting me on the butt and rubbing his body close to mine. He placed a piece of paper in my hand and whispered, "Put it away." It was his telephone number to call him. He had been warned many of times about trying to see me behind Reverend Smith's back but he was still trying.

Years later (after I had given up the lifestyle) I was teaching at a school where I taught Reverend Hale's niece. She was a very nice, smart and athletic little girl. Her mother was gunned down. I went to the house to show my respect after the tragedy. I had no idea I was going to see her uncle and he would still be up to "game." Anyway, I did go out to be with him at the Crowne Plaza. I had my car valet parked as I had always done. There he was in the room drinking gin, taking blood pressure medication and trying to still get me to join his church, help write a proposal and work under his wife's leadership. What a fool!

Then to top it all off, he offered me $50. By then, my life had changed. I told him I was a minister myself and that I could write my own proposal. I told him he must have been smoking crack and I must have looked like the same little stupid girl I was many years ago. He started begging and pleading to never let that night go any further than there. He said, "Please do not tell Reverend Smith." I was glad to tell him my life was far past being a little "Miss It" for them. I told him that his friend would find out about him one day and all of them would end up in hell together paying for hotels and screwing young girls. He looked at me with a funny expression on his face and I exited. I have never looked back.

Before I was liberated from this lifestyle, I'm sure you're wondering why I continued to go back. Being 17-years-old, carrying a secret and getting paid cash to get what I wanted was not so bad. Pastor Smith had become my drug. He was a walking aphrodisiac. I was getting addicted to fast life. He was making me believe he loved me. He had me believing that he cared so much for me that he would hurt someone if he saw me with them. I was free to drink alcoholic beverages, blaze up a joint that was rolled for me and just be loose and fancy free. He brainwashed me into believing, "After all, if Pastor is doing this, it's okay for me too." I had no idea I had to give an account for my own actions. I am ever grateful today, though, that the Lord did make me realize that I would soon have to turn from my evil ways.

Chapter 14

Stressful Events

On February 23, 1978, my paternal grandmother passed away. She was ill and did not want the family in California to know it. I had an odd feeling about her. She always would send me a fruitcake. Christmas came and nothing arrived, not even a telephone call. I could not locate her. My birthday came and no card arrived. I called her day and night, but got no answer. I knew she did 'day work,' better known as housekeeping, but certainly not all day and all night. I called my daddy. He just talked, but never did he tell me Ma Bonnie was ill. I started calling hospitals. There were only a few in 1978.

I called each one of them and asked if they had a patient called Bonnie Morrison and found her in intensive care. I asked the nurse to please put the telephone to her ear and let me talk to her. I was calling long distance from California. I was her granddaughter. I needed to talk to her. It was February 22, 1978. I told her I loved her very much, and I missed her. Strangely, I felt real funny. The fruitcakes she would send to me felt special and I never ate them because I really did not like them but I never told her. I know she did certain things to make the cakes special. But I just did not or do not still today like fruitcakes. I knew I was not going to get anymore when I heard her voice. I wanted to just scream, holler and cry. Today I wish I just had just the smell of that fruitcake.

To my amazement, she was short of breath, but she told me she loved me, too. She told me to take care of my little girl and to take care of myself. We hung up. I never told her I was pregnant with my second child.

The same day, Jaray and I had an argument over me going to see my grandmother. He said, "No." During the course of the argument, he kicked the telephone off the receiver and dared me to put it back on. Marilyn's fourth birthday was the very next day, and I had planned a birthday party for her at her school.

Early on the 24th of February, my mother came to my house and said she had been trying to call me all night and that the line was busy. She tried to have the operator place an emergency call to release the line, but the operator told her the telephone was off the receiver.

My mother also said my Aunt Sicily from Baton Rouge was trying to call me to tell me Ma Bonnie had passed. I started crying. I was so sad. Jaray showed no remorse. My mother advised me to go on with Marilyn's 4th birthday party and I did. When I got home from the birthday party, I asked Jaray if he would go with me to my grandmother's funeral but he refused. He started an argument about any and every little thing. I was six months pregnant with my Jaray, Jr. at that time. My feelings were very delicate plus now my Ma Bonnie was gone and I was hurting deeply and Jaray was acting like a cold-hearted mammal. I asked my younger brother, Aston, would he fly out there with me. He said, "Yes."

When we arrived in Baton Rouge, Aston and I stayed at my stepmother's house, which was right down the street from Ma Bonnie's house. All of Ma Bonnie's sisters and brothers stayed at her house. Aston and I stayed in the same room. I slept in the bed and Aston slept in a chair all night. He was protecting me to see if I was going to be okay.

My daddy very specifically told me I was not to do or say anything about the funeral. My Aunt Sicily and Ma Bonnie were very close. I was to let Aunt Sicily handle everything and keep my mouth closed. "Do you understand," my daddy asked me.

I said, "Yes." Aunt Sicily handled everything. She did an excellent job. Ma Bonnie's sisters and cousins came from San Francisco, and they were hurt and sad because they did not know she was so sick. It was Ma Bonnie's wishes not to bother any relatives with her illness. My grandmother was so neat and clean. All of her things just had to be labeled and boxed. Of course, there were relatives picking up items and talking about what they wanted. My Aunt Sicily gave instructions from Ma Bonnie. She had a will. Still people will do what they want to do, but there was no fighting or arguing just stealing.

Ma Bonnie was a very classy lady. Everything she wore was coordinated. Believe it or not, Bonnie Morrison was a very intelligent lady. She had three or four different bank accounts with money in them. She had insurance policies and everything was paid for in her home.

She left that beautiful home to her son, my daddy, and my God what a blessing that was to him. He never moved in the house nor did he take full advantage of all the furniture in the house. At that time, Daddy was still a rolling stone. Like the Temptations' song said, "Wherever he left his hat was his home." And now that he is old and sick, all he is alone.

In August 1986, death hit again. "Oh, my God," I thought. "That precious woman who kept our maternal family together was gone." Grandma Mary provided us with true unity. All major holidays, we ate as a family and Grandma Mary led the prayer. She kept her children, her grandchildren and she kept her great-grandchildren. I did an article about her in the *Sentinel* newspaper. What a great woman she was, a sharecropper, and after the life and death of my grandfather, Pa Pa, she never remarried. She raised all five of her children alone with Jesus. All of her children went to college. Grandma washed and ironed for all of us. She treated each one of us special. She was a very good woman, but when she said something she meant it. She spoke what was on her mind. She did not believe in spoiling the child and sparing the rod. She whipped our asses when we were young and she carried her gun in her apron pocket and would remind us that she would shoot us if we disrespected her. She did not go for the craziness from her children, grandchildren or great grandchildren. Grandma Mary got nothing but respect from us. If we said something it was under our breath where we only could hear ourselves.

After spending many wonderful years with Grandma Mary, she started telling us about a severe pain she had in her side. I remember praying for her healing once, just the two of us. There were other members of the family that she told about this pain she was experiencing in her side. Shortly after that, Grandma Mary was admitted to the St. Francis Hospital, in Lynnwood, California, and diagnosed with advanced pancreatic cancer. She passed away, at eighty-two (82) years old and it was like, "**WOW, the ROOT is gone.**" There was a dinner at Christmas again, but it was not the same. My mother and aunts and uncle tried to go on with the dinner despite her absence. I just did not want to be there. I prayed and prayed. God, please help me. I don't want to be at the family dinner without Grandma Mary.

Some of my friends were Masons and Eastern Stars. They were selling raffle tickets. 1st prize was a trip to Hawaii on December 25, 1986 2nd prize was $50.00 and 3rd prize was $25.00. Anyway, I bought a few tickets. My thoughts were, "What the hell, it's only a dollar." Guess what? I won the trip to Hawaii. It was a trip for two. All expenses were paid. I did not have to remain in the Los Angeles dealing with my grief at Grandma's house.

I invited the school police, Walter Nelson, from my job to go on vacation with me. He did. He was paranoid the whole time like he was on police duty. He never relaxed. My girlfriend Ida invited us to her home. She has a lovely home near the beach. We had dinner and she had it laid out so beautiful. Her beautiful china was trimmed in gold. She served Hors d'oeuvres and red wine. Her main course was Turkey, Brisket, dressing, greens, potato salad, potato pies, and pineapples. After we ate, we all went to the beach on Christmas Day. It was a beautiful sunshiny day. There I was on the beach in Hawaii, enjoying 80-degree weather and trying to overcome some of my grief. It was working.

Later, my mother and my aunts decided they would open a school and church together. My children, my oldest brother, Sam, Jr.'s children, my aunt's son, and others attended the school. There was soooooo much love and cohesiveness among us. We were trying to keep it together in the midst of feeling the great loss of Grandma Mary. But, there was nothing to fill the void that we felt from our loss.

More stress came in 1988. My daughter was attending Westchester High School. While she was leaving the dressing area in the P.E. room, the door closure fell on top of her head. She ended up getting her hair cut out and stitches put in. She was placed on home schooling and while this drama was unfolding, my oldest brother, Sam, Jr. became very ill. He was such a beautiful person with a pleasant personality. He was ill and hid it. He was a Viet Nam veteran of the USMC (United States Marine Corp) On February 8th, someone called the school office and informed me that my brother was very ill and had been hospitalized in intensive care at Martin Luther King Hospital. The assistant principal, Dr. Bennett, came very quietly to my office and told me. He was so gracious that he had another employee drive me to the hospital. Sam, Jr. would always say he did not want to live anymore after Grandma Mary passed.

I could not believe my eyes. I loved my brother so much. He was the green-eyed monster with whom I always got in trouble. We loved each other. We had chicken pox together. We sold peanuts, competing to see who could sell the most. (Our dad used to poach peanuts since he was 12/13 years-old and he still does. He's now 86-years-old). We competed to see who could make the better grades, which could make the better grades, which could play the most musical instruments. He really got me when he was in the Marines. He took me to a concert and introduced me to one of his band member friends. Later that night, he told me he had sold my clarinet to this guy. I could not even get angry. Sam, Jr. had so much charisma. Unfortunately, his wife left him, taking their three daughters at the time of his illness and returned to her hometown in New Jersey. It was not my business to ask why. I did know she needed to be aware of how sick my brother was.

We called her father and told him if she called, please have her call us immediately because her husband was in intensive care. Cell phones were not as common then as they are now. RoxAnn (his wife) did call but she refused to come back. Well, on Friday, February 13, 1989, Sam, Jr. passed away. I will never forget; it was about 11:30 p.m.My three children were in the bed with me when three clouds of smoke came into my room. I got up and rushed to the telephone and called the hospital and asked had his status in the coma been changed. They told me to call back. They were working on him. I woke my daddy up; he had flown out from Baton Rouge to see him. We had gone to the hospital earlier, and when Daddy told Jr., "Blow that saxophone," Jr. moved his head from side to side. We just knew he was going to make a comeback. I told Daddy what happened to me with the clouds of smoke. By the time I had finished telling him the telephone rang and asked us to bring the family in. We got ready and went to the hospital. They called us in the conference room and told us when I called they were trying to save him. He passed away. They walked us into the room. Aston grabbed Jr. and cried and cried. We called Momma. She was very sad. We all were very sad. My brother's death was so sudden, so unexpected. Sam, Jr.'s wife and daughters had arrived in New Jersey. When they got the news, RoxAnn said they could not afford to come back. Daddy called his wife and told her to give me the credit card number. I called the airlines and Jr.'s wife and three daughters had a chance to view him one last time. Their oldest daughter hollered and cried the entire homegoing service.

After the homegoing services, the children never came back to Southern California again. It amazes me. My mother was extremely a big help to my nieces and my sister-in-law when they lived in California. The children attended school and RoxAnn was employed by my mother. Still to this day, both of my parents are still waiting for a simple telephone call to hear from them.

When Sam, Jr. passed away, Aston was totally lost. The two brothers were very close. Aston's life really turned all the way down. He turned to the streets. Once he came to my job and demanded money. He had a gun and he intended to shoot me. I screamed, "Lord, help me."

Six years later, Friday, January 13, 1995, my uncle, Harvey died seven days after his birthday. My uncle was a prominent minister in Baton Rouge, Louisiana. My mother could not attend the funeral because my stepfather was awaiting a heart transplant. He had experienced some heart attacks and was even being hospitalized shortly before my uncle's death. My uncle and my stepfather had a very good relationship. Mother told me to not mention the death of her brother to her husband.

While I was preparing for the home going services of my uncle, my stepfather had a stroke that caused him to be paralyzed. He was hospitalized. After the series of strokes, the heart transplant was history.

His other sisters did not attend his home going services either. Nieces and nephews attended from all over the United States. He had cousins and numerous Pastors attend his services. They held his services at the convention center in Baton Rouge. At that time the family from the West Coast asked me to speak on their behalf at the services. After the services, my younger brother, Aston, went through some real drama. People were on his back since all our first cousins felt they deserved a portion of the inheritance. Our uncle had no children and he had three surviving sisters who gave their share of inheritance to Aston since he took care of Uncle Harvey the last few years of his life.

Then, just three months later on Sunday, April 2, 1995, my stepfather passed away in Daniel Freeman Hospital. He had had many strokes since January and his heart just gave out. He was a very good daddy to me. I loved him very much. He and my mother were a perfect couple. They used to go to church together, go fishing together, play cards, and break bread together. He loved barbequing. I did not think he and Momma knew each other's name. He called her "Baby," and she called him "Honey." One day I even asked them if they knew each other's real name.

When they got married, my stepfather had three children of his own, and Momma had the three of us. We were the Brady Bunch. All of us were close in age. We got along as well as could be; Daddy and Momma did not let us interfere with their relationship. They helped each one of us as parents who care would. When Daddy passed away, my stepsister and I were at his bedside. We gave him his last communion, and then he took his last breath.

After his death, an ugly drama started at church. His children wanted to know what he left for them. Only one of them did not. Believe it or not they actually hired a paralegal to investigate. I was served papers. Did they not realize I was on the same level as they were? I was one of the children also. The officiating minister offered to read the will after the service, but they refused. He left perfect, clear cut instructions.

God, help me, Jesus. July 26, 2002 came and also the death of my darling baby Jaray, Jr. Oh my God, my God. The deaths of all my dear, sweet, loved ones hurt, but Lord, when my child, my son, my baby was shot three time to death, it took life out of me. This seemed like all I could take. In my wildest imagination, I never dreamed of burying any of my children. I was numb, vulnerable, and broken. I found out that people will get you when your guards are down. Not strangers, but very close relatives. There were so many people. My son knew everybody, it seemed. One of my ex-husbands (Jaray, Sr.) talked to me. He said that we should just put whatever had happened to us in the past behind us. **YEA, RIGHT!!!!!!** When we got to the mortuary, he wanted to go as cheap as possible and even buy a feminine casket. He asked the counselor how anyone could tell the difference. I flew off the deep end. My daughter-in-law was there. She was also offended. I informed the counselor that I wanted the best for my baby. He lived a masculine, classy life, and I wanted him to leave in a masculine, classy finale. He was not living on "the down low" nor was he going to buried that way. Because of my stern feelings about the burial of my son, Jaray, Sr. gave absolutely no money at all toward the funeral. He got a limo for himself and his out of town family, which was his mother, sisters, his other daughter, and brother. He did not contribute anything toward the family flowers. **BUT** he **did** collect on the life insurance policy on my son. One of my friends always reminds me that God sits high, and he looks low. He does not slumber nor sleep. He was buried August 2002 and thank you, JESUS, my last payment was paid in full January 2005.

His mother came to the city for the first time in her life, and not once did she call me. However, I did get a message through Jaray that she wanted to say a few words at the services. She greeted me from the pulpit with a "Hello to my sister in Christ." That was in the church.

There was women drama. My first grandson, James, by Jaray and his mother were there from Arkansas. My daughter-in-law was there with her and Jaray's daughter, Sara. She had just turned one-year-old the day before we buried her daddy. Drama- James' momma kept introducing herself as Jaray's girlfriend and Sara's momma was so angry she had nothing nice at all to say about her husband (Jaray).

Marilyn was freaking out because she wanted to style her brother's hair for the service. She had styled hair many times for mortuaries but the mortuary counselor told her this would be totally different. Her brother had suffered two gun shot wounds to his head and it was not anything nice to see if you are close relatives. This would be different. This was her brother. She screamed and hollered and cried how she and her brothers had discussed their last wishes with each other. I did not want a dysfunctional daughter as well as a deceased son so I had to say," No" and put my foot down.

Mark just stayed real quite and attentive to me and his little sister, Ebony. That kind of bothered me. He was not facing what had just happened. Jaray and Mark were like two peas in a pod. Ebony would cry out how much she was going to miss her Jaray, Jr.

My newly wed husband, Jake, was too busy trying to let the world know we were married. We had just gotten married on July 9. (Jaray, Jr. was murdered July 26th). He was really working my nerves. He was not the center stage of attention. Did he not know I had lost my son that had been in the world with me for 24 years and I had only known him maybe a couple of years if that long?

The day of the homegoing, I know my baby's services were so beautifully and orderly done. My friend, the late Bishop Ralph Artiaga, officiated. So many people came to honor Jaray, Jr. There were so many people. My son loved people and it showed. God has no respect of a person and I must say Jaray, Jr. did not either. It seemed like everyone was there. Limos were given to the family and Jackson limo gave me a private limo along with the two that came with the services.

Thank you to the young lady that handed me $20.00 she had gotten from Jaray, Jr. the day he was murdered. I still have it. I don't know you but I can still hear your voice telling me to take the $20.00 and keep it.

I want to thank the pastor who allowed us to use the neighborhood church to eulogize Jaray, Jr. It allowed so many of his acquaintances and his friends to walk to the service. We had lived in the neighborhood since he was a year old. Jaray, Jr. was such a charmer and a friendly person.

We had the repast at the church where I was the founder and pastor for the past 13 years. It was wonderful. So many wonderful people, including family and friends were there. Jaray and his family went and had their separate repast at his home in Compton.
I want to thank the Burroughs family for the catering and so much food. You were excellent. Again thank you EJ for my personal limo and for my extended family.

As I sat in church trying to be as normal as I could be, talking to people that I had not seen for a long time, that newlywed husband of mine kept calling me on the cell phone to leave the repast and come sit in the limo with him. **Was that a sick person or what?** I answered a few times but then I stopped. He was working my last nerves. You would think he would have shown some compassion during that horrible time. The straw that really broke the camel's back occurred when we were in the Inglewood Cemetery. He actually told me my grieving should end the day of the service.

Stress continues, with my Daddy, Sam who has lived the true good life. How his present family is making sure of it. For all of his life, he has gone by his name and birthday July 22, 1922 and just this year in his declining years of Alzheimer's, his beloved wife has decided to change his birthday to a different month and day. What is the purpose? He has no idea what's going on.

Chapter 15
Marriages Not Ordained by God

"What therefore God hath joined together, let no man put asunder."

(Matthew 19:6)

Often people put themselves together in marriage, not God. In my life, I have suffered a severe problem with that issue. I had a problem. I wanted to be married with lovely children. There was a problem. I did not wait on God; neither did I let God ordain the marriages. I did it. I do mean "**I.**" What a mess I made of my life. I have no one to blame but me. Here we go: five marriages and guess what? None today.

I married my high school male friend when I was 18-years-old. I was trying to be a "miss smart ass" and eloped with him. I wanted to be married wearing a big diamond, have children, live in a nice home and drive a nice car. Of course, my dream was for us to go to church, go out and party together, have friends that had the same common goals, be two hard working people with early retirement in mind, treating me as I am his precious queen, and he my king, have a dog for a pet and just be in love with each other and be happy. By the time the marriage ended, I felt like my ass had been through a ringer. All things I had dreamed of were not the dream of this man that I married. He and the other four men I chose had another agenda. Ladies and gentlemen, I am here to tell you, **YOU cannot change anyone but yourself**. Like Sam Cook says, "I know my change is gonna come, oh yes it is. It's been too hard of living but I'm afraid to die. I don't know what's up there beyond the sky."

2nd Marriage

I remarried again in August 1984 and divorced exactly one year later. We both were at the same time filing for a divorce. He persistently chased me on my job. I had recently changed schools and was very depressed. Believe it or not, after being in a relationship for 12 years is not like a water faucet that you can turn on and off. My heart was trying hard to be in this relationship but it was not reciprocated.

Whoa! One spring day, my 10th grade reading class was sitting down acting out a play . I had a professional teacher's assistant that helped me in the class. Here comes this good looking tall chocolate brown handsome man with a beard and a mustache. He came in my classroom to fix a lock on my desk. When he approached my desk, I quickly jumped up. I did not even want him to accidentally touch me. I was very standoffish. Anyway, he told me he would have to come back to finish the lock. I said, "Okay," and he said,"Good day."

When he came back and secured the lock on my desk, he asked me out on a lunch date. I immediately said, "No." I said, "There's my assistant."

She immediately said, "Oh, you can take me to McDonald's, Jack in the Box or just anywhere. You are so fine."

He said, "Alright." He did take her to McDonald's. She came back and told me, "Girl, he is so fine I would have him any day." He told me he had to do something to my door closure. He would be back. I said, "Yeah."

On his return to repair the door closure, he very smoothly said, "Hello there."

I responded, "Hi, how are you?"

He told me he was okay.

I told him I was blessed. I asked him did he do work on the side.

He said yes, he did.

I asked him for his telephone number and he gave me his pager number and the rest is what you call history.

He came over and changed all my locks to fit one key. I just thought this was simply amazing. He met my children. My baby, Mark, was still in diapers crawling around trying to make steps. He picked him up and played with him. Mark was a baby with a lot of personality. He just laughed with him. I bathed my children and put them to bed. Mr. Fine, better known as Larry, had brought a six-pack of Miller Beer. He was drinking by himself until I put the children to bed, and then I joined him. He had bought some medium red wine. We drank and talked way past my sleep time. I did not know that fixing my locks were going to keep me awake that long. He finally left. I was very sleepy the next morning as I tried to get the children ready for school the next day.

I soon learned he liked the simple things of life. Things that I liked also such as attending church, going to the beach biking, sitting outside in the backyard kicking it, taking a ride in the car, taking a trip to the mountains and camping out were real cool with him, too. What was really cool was the fact that he did things that included my children.

We had a problem. I refused to allow him to sleep with me and disrespect my children in our home. He was very kind to my Grandma Mary, my mother, actually to my entire family. We used to take Grandma Mary to the beach with us. Soon it came to okay, but I began to feel like, "If it's going to be this serious, we need to make a commitment." He agreed but never did the asking or suggesting that we should become one. He knew I had baggage. I had just divorced, I was a proud mother of three children and that was not just going to go into a magic hat and disappear.

Soon he told me about him having a son around the same age as Mark and a very bad case of baby momma drama. She wanted to be his wife and she wanted him to care for the child and have visitation but she must be included all the time in the visits. Not only that, he told me about another older woman he was living with on and off. He told me where she lived. He said it was over between them.

He soon introduced me to his lovely mother, sisters and brothers. I was in awe. His niece was one of my students when I taught Journalism and English/Language Arts in a middle school in South Central Los Angeles.

After we had gone through a few drama scenes from both sides, we had to have some serious talks. Larry and I had attempted to take the children to Jaray one Friday night and he pulled a gun on me and asked me if I wanted trouble. The suggestion was he was not keeping the children on that weekend he had so diligently asked the judge for. We did a u-turn in the middle of Vermont Avenue, took the children and got the hell away from Jaray's apartment.

Larry's baby momma knew I was not going for the bullshit she was trying to pull. She did not want the child at my house. She wanted Larry to come to her house every week and spend time with their child so she could entertain him. He could not or maybe did not want to believe she was playing games that he enjoyed.

After we got married, August 1984, real drama started unfolding. Let the games begin. It took every bit of one year for us to not want to be husband and wife anymore. Larry and I had some real good times. I would see him all the time, day and evening. I was a high school counselor and he was a locksmith. My school was one of the schools he serviced. Larry could do anything. He could build, he could put any and everything together, and he could paint. He could not cook. I loved to cook. My how perfect was this man. I would get a hug, a kiss, gentle touches, massages, (even my feet) and he even took it upon himself to take Mark to the babysitter everyday. He referred to Mark as "packman." I took Jaray and Marilyn to school. We took our lunch breaks together and we would have lunch everyday in Exposition Park. He had a blue van and he would pick me up each day and drop me back off to work.

Man, lunch was most of the time just the simple things of life like being together and sharing thoughts. I think if he had his choosing, sex would come before food. I accommodated my spouse. He had the sexiest voice, "Hello there." He would refer to me as being his Tonka Toy and he was my Tin Man. We would go to the beach after work and let the children ride bikes and we picnicked in the sand. He helped the children make sand castles. We just had fun. We had juice for the children and beer for us in the cooler and sandwiches for us. We went to the mountains with the children, too. He let them slide down the hills in snow. We had the fireplace on. I was cooking and he was playing with Marilyn, Jaray, Jr. and Mark. The kids had hot chocolate and we had brandy.

Soon Larry started getting late calls in the night. I knew his job required late calls so I had no problems with that. Sometimes he would go and come right back and sometimes he would take hours. Most of the time he did not want to discuss where he had been or either he would tell me he was by one of his sisters' house or at his mother's house.

Sometimes I would go on some of the calls. I sometimes did not believe his customers. Women would open the door in their negligee with breasts hanging out. I would walk in with him and stare at their breasts and their attire the whole time he would be working on locks. I thought, "Damn, they knew he was coming but for what? A seduction or working on locks?" I started asking him not to go after a certain hour. He insisted that was his job, so he had to go when he was called.

We went on a nice cruise to Catalina. We enjoyed every minute. We both loved the water, bicycling and playing the videogame, Pacman. We relaxed and prepared to return home. The very next weekend he was MIA (missing in action). I went bananas. He told me he was trying to help some lady fix a lock on Santa Monica Boulevard and the police took him to jail. Soooooooooooo not true. He was caught soliciting a prostitute that turned out to be a female police on Santa Monica Boulevard. They sent the report in the mail. I was just baffled. This is a man that I made sex available to whenever he wanted. I found that he started lying to me. He would stutter and I would say, "Awe shit! Here goes another damn lie." Things started getting worse than better.

One Friday evening he did not come home. We used to follow each other from work. He would come and wait for me and follow me home. If someone would pull in the middle of us, he would pull over and there we would be tailgating smiling with each other until we arrived home. I decided to put my Mark in the car and take a ride toward the Wilshire/ Robertson area where he had told me he used to date the older other woman. It was a dark nice evening. I was nervous but I needed to know what the hell was going on. It was my intuition that there was someone else in the picture. It was in my gut. I wanted to know if he had returned to someone that he said he was through with. Yet while we were still married, he always spoke of expensive trips and conventions trips they had taken, how much fun they had over seas, and how much money she owed him.

Mark was on the back seat asleep when I arrived into this quite neighborhood and saw his van parked in front of her door. I parked across the driveway for a few minutes and took a deep breath. I looked down the driveway. There he was in a workshed area sawing some type of wood. This was the saw I had bought for this man and there he was making something for this bit—. I got out of the car and rang her doorbell. An older bent over, oversized, red short haired, wrinkled woman came to the door and said, "Yes?"

I said, "I would like to see Larry."

She said, "Who wants him?"

I said, "His wife."

Her big dog was barking fiercely and she let the dog come at me. By that time Larry came to the door. I told him, "Get that damn dog, don't let it bite me," and, "Why in the hell are you here?" He was closing the door behind him and she was just standing there. I said, "I sure in the hell hope that is Joanie's momma and not her or man you are insane. You are cheating on my beautiful black ass for that old stinky broad?"

He did not answer. I jumped in my car and started banging his van with my Honda wagon. I was hurt and mad as hell. This man whom

I thought to be so damn attentive to me was cheating on me and lying about side jobs. He came to the window and grabbed my neck. And I put the car in first and was dragging his ass down the street. The white folks had gotten a scene that night. After that we both went to separate paralegals and that was the end of that marriage.

After we both had cooled off, he started calling me again but the marriage was over and he was still doing the same shit: calling me and still had Ms. Joanie. How do I know this? Right after my grandmother died in 1986, his brother passed. My brother passed in February 1989 and his mother passed July 4, 1989. He called me to let me know. When I saw the obituary, Ms. Joanie was in charge as being the companion. He did the closing music (the Commodores) for my brother's services.

Later, he got married to a sister. They moved right down the street from me. According to one of his sisters, he was not supposed to come in front of my house. Oh well, Larry still came over and did anything I asked of him until the day I left. His current wife probably has the patience for the bullshit. She has even called this house. Ladies remind you that callers ID do exist. I was shocked to get a telephone call from her. She doesn't trust his ass either if she's calling long distance to check. All I can say to her is, "Don't worry about me, little lady. It's over because the fat lady has sung." In my eyes he is still the nice man. Even though he had a few hang-ups, I did love him very much.

Here was my excuse to return to "Spiritual Seduction." Century Boulevard was hot again for Angela.

3ʳᵈ Marriage

August 1986, two of my friends and I decided to take a trip to Jamaica. I was a divorced woman and I thought I would change my hair color. I did not know what to expect. Both of the ladies I was traveling with were about 16 years older than me. I knew I was going to be protected. Well, we traveled on Delta Air Lines and had a layover in Miami. When we landed in Jamaica, we stayed in this lady's villa that Robin knew. It was Robin, Rita, and me. Jacklyn picked us up from the airport and showed us around the villa. It was a very big house. Robin, Rita, and I shared the same room. The weather felt like velvet.

Jacklyn took us on a tour and we bought souvenirs. She had a pool. I knew nothing about swimming but I would get out at the pool and have fun. One day some policemen came to the villa and I was introduced to one. His name was Charles.

Charles asked me to go riding with him on his motorcycle. I declined. It was a little too much for me. He came back and got me in the car. That day we went to a hut where they served jerk chicken, jerk pork, and rum punch. The food was excellent and the rum punched slipped up right on me.

I told Charles I was ready to go home so he told me he would take me if I promised to go out dancing with him that night. I obliged. I took a nap and freshened up for the night.

We had so much fun at the club dancing. He taught me how to sway my hips back and forth and get in the groove with the other people on the floor dancing. I had so much fun that night. I was up dancing on every song.

During the whole seven days I was there, Charles saw to it that I had a good time and that I had a chance to tour many sites that I would not have had a chance to see otherwise.

At the end of the trip, Charles asked me for my telephone number. He took us back to the airport reluctantly because he wanted me to stay. I told him I had a job and three children. I was just on vacation. If things went well, I would return.

We called each other everyday, day and night. Until yours truly (Stella) thought I would get my groove back. We talked about him coming to the United States. That was all good. Then we talked about getting married. Wow, he was so much younger than me. I was ten years older than him.

We made plans to get married that November. I went and bought a beautiful wedding dress and one of Los Angeles' radio stations came and deejayed the wedding reception. We had to go through a whole little routine that they had to do before marriage. I was not fond of it but here I was in some shit I really was not sure I wanted to be in. Rita came back with me to be my matron of honor. Also, one of the guys there showed a lot of interest in her.

The wedding was on a beautiful sunny day on top of a mountain with green background. It was a private wedding with only Charles, his best man, Rita and me. The reception was later that evening. Whoever planned the reception, it was the greatest. Charles had so many relatives and friends. The deejay from Los Angeles had it on and popping all night long. Everything was fine until I heard Charles bragging to his friends in his language that he had no plans to stay with me once he came to the United States. I played it off the rest of the night but I never confronted him or said anything.

When Rita and I got back on the airplane, I told her. When I arrived home, he called me several times, but I told him I did not think it was a good idea. I filed for a divorce immediately.

This here Stella ended her groove real quick. All was not lost, though, because I did learn how to make rum punch and Jamaican fish.

4th Marriage

Okay! I had started into turn to a real introvert. I had gone through drama with my aunt over a court case. I was Mom's taxi, taking Jaray, Jr. to a middle school, Mark to an elementary school and Marilyn to the school where a very polite man worked. His name was Ray.

He would make it his business to come out and be very courteous to me. Some days I would be walking around the school track exercising, praying and picking up cans and bottles. Yes, call me a bag lady but I was leaning and depending on Jesus.

He asked me for my telephone number. I gave it to him. It was getting close to Christmas and he called me and asked me what my address was. Funny enough I tried to be, I gave him my post office box number. He said, "May I have your address where you reside?" About an hour later, he came over. Mark was very upset. He told him he could not come in. No man was going to pimp his mother. I should have listened to my young child. He saw something I could not see.

He had many late nights at my home and insisted and asked me to marry him. We did get married but my......my......my how I went through woman after woman calling me. I was constantly being disrespected by some of his young female students and it goes on.

He was kind to Jaray, Jr., Mark, and me. My sons liked him very much. I can say he really took care of my children financially and made sure I had everything I needed. Marilyn was away in college and he would get up in the middle of the night to wire her money if she needed it.

When Lil Ebony came, you would have thought she was the princess. Ray thought she was God's gift to the world. Lil Ebony was only two-months-old and he bought her a separate turkey. Her first Christmas, she had her own personal Christmas tree in her room. For her first birthday, he hired Tommy the Clown. It went on and on with Ebony getting elaborate gifts. She was getting manicures and pedicures at age two. Her little nails weren't even ready for all of this. But Ray and his daughter were running hard together. What did I do to spoil of this fine action? I told Ebony her daddy was a dog and at the age of two, she waited until they were in the grocery store, and said, "Daddy, Mommy called you a dog." He turned around and people were looking at him and all he could do was say, "**Ruff ...... Ruff.**"

What Lil Ebony did not realize was that Daddy was leaving when she went to sleep telling me he had to go to work at 3:00 a.m. Don't you know I was being played big time? Yes, Ray had other women.

When I found out, I had changed my life. The evil spirit of being seduced by the Pastors and friends were all over. There were no more telephone calls to Reverend Smith. I prayed more and read the word for knowledge and understanding. I knew how good God is, had been and was gonna be.

I filed for divorce and Ray tried to stop it in all ways that he could. This is when I, indeed, knew that God is my all and all. He told me he was going to cut me off of everything and he did. This included Lil Ebony. She had to become a part of the financial cutoff. All of Daddy's love had to end. It was his way of making me beg him back. Thanks to God's grace, I'm happy that one is over.

We had a lot of wonderful days but, unfortunately, he had a weakness for ladies. I thank God I am away from that bondage.

5th Marriage

What a short and not so sweet one. I was actually married to the preacher. I had all signs when we were dating that Joseph was cheap but I did not adhere to the flags. When we went out to dinner at the "Sizzler" restaurant, he would purchase one meal and we—-all three, Ebony, him, and I—-would eat off the same plate. I thought it was romantic at first but then later on I didn't think anything was cute about it.

I would ask him to take over church some Sundays when I was tired but he would tell me he wasn't the pastor, I was.

He was very religious. Church was not an option. He wanted to be there at His church, seven days out of seven. Nothing is wrong with that but even the Holy Word says there is a time and season for all things (Ecclesiastes. 3:1). Everyone needs balance in their life.

What really tore my heart apart was the day of my Jaray, Jr.'s homegoing services. He told me my grief should end in the cemetery. I had only known this man a couple of years and had only been married to him from July 9th – Aug. 8th. I do know that if any of these marriages would have been ordained by God, I would still be happily married. I realized that I was not in God's Will.

Chapter 16

Woman, Thou Art Loosed

I stayed in this formidable lifestyle for more than 15 years. Wow, what a waste. What a shame. What a myriad of poor decisions. Yes, the lifestyle was good. I believe I had gotten totally spoiled. But as I went on from day to day, I couldn't help but remember the teachings I'd been taught as a little girl. The Bible teaches that you should train up a child in the way, in which they should go, when they are older, they won't depart (Proverbs 22:6). In other words, if you train a child up by teaching them right from wrong, especially as it relates to the things of God, they may stray for a while, but they will eventually come back to their senses. So it was with me.

I spent a lot of time in the earlier chapters describing what my upbringing was like. I was introduced to Jesus early in life by my momma and by my grandma. But just like many other young girls who come from good, church going, God-fearing families, I got caught up. After being in the lifestyle for over 15 years, something began to tug me on the inside. I started noticing "withdrawal symptoms" around this time. I would seek opportunities to make my time with Big Daddy very short. There were even times when I would say, "I'm going to the restroom" and I wouldn't come back. There were other times when I wouldn't show up for an escapade. I wouldn't even call; I was a no-show. Because that had become a periodic routine, I had already been given the nickname, Runaway.

Every time I made up my mind to leave and leave for good, Big Daddy would always say something intimidating that would scare me into staying. "Aww, girl. you know you need me. You know you want this money. You know ain't nobody gonna do it to you like Big Daddy do it to you. We got a good thing going on, girl. Why you gonna be like that?"

The more he begged and complained, the more he drew me in. I heard him, but something in my heart just didn't feel right. The fact that I began to mature and realize I really was wrong helped me to get through this as well. I was particularly frightened when some tragedies took place involving other pastors whose promiscuous extra-marital affairs began to be exposed. Little by little, day by day, I began to wonder, "Girl, how'd you get here? You've got to get out of this lifestyle. Don't you know this is somebody's husband? Don't you know his wife can come up in here and blow your head off at any moment's notice? What will you say to your mother and father? How will you explain this to your children?"

The questions kept coming at me like a kid throwing a snowball at a playmate. I just didn't know what to do. I felt so little. I felt like I had done so much wrong that God would never forgive me. I felt like I was a bad person. I felt like I was at the bottom of the barrel and there was no hope for me. I felt like according to Hebrews 10:26, I would never be forgiven because I had willfully continued to sin after I had received knowledge of what was right and what was wrong.

But here's the good news. The Bible declares that if we would confess our sins before the Lord, He is faithful to forgive us of our sins. I began to search the scriptures because I knew that faith comes by hearing and hearing by the Word of God. I began to remember the many scriptures I heard about God's love and forgiveness, and I knew that this was what I wanted in my life.

Another liberating factor was Academy Cathedral. After so much folly with Reverend Smith, there was no way I could continue to go to church with him and take him seriously. How could I? The more I sat under the pastor at Academy Cathedral, the more I began to come into the knowledge that God could set me free. I learned so much under his teaching. There's one thing I learned for sure: God can deliver anybody from anything if they desire to be delivered. I don't care if it's drugs, alcohol, promiscuity, homosexuality, a lying tongue, thieving hands—-whatever. Deliverance is available. Thank you Jesus!

For many years, I listened to several preachers preach and some even taught. I was so blessed that God saved ME. I sang in the choir, was a Sunday School teacher, a youth supervisor, spoke at women's programs, got some valuable pulpit experience in the 70's at my uncle's church, and was a faithful doorkeeper (usher).

God has blessed all of us with an anointing. All we have to do is pray and have faith.

I give all the praise and honor to Him. Later in the late 80's and early 90's, again, I was an usher and enjoyed it. I attended church every day. My immediate family told me I was going to get burned out. "Stop being a fanatic," they jeered. But they just did not understand what was happening to me. I was being transformed. In the midst of coming out of my shameful lifestyle, I was becoming a new creature in Christ Jesus and I was enjoying it. When I went to bed at night, I would finally experience **the peace of God, which passeth all understanding (Philippians 4:7).**

Again, I learned a lot from the pastor and elders at Academy Cathedral. The Word was taught and it made a tremendous impact on my life. By this time, I had children, and it meant a lot to be a part of a church family that offered family activities. On Monday nights the children could play video games, basketball, and socialize after they had an hour of Bible Study. They had Bible Study for adults, too. On Tuesday, there was a midday service that was always so refreshing, and on Wednesdays we had midweek services in the evenings. I was there every chance I could get. There was always something to learn. This was when I was finding out "oh much I love Jesus."

It was good to discover how Jesus has no respect of a person. He's the sweetest person I know. Sure enough, can't nobody do me like Jesus. I know that He is my friend. I was having such a Holy Ghost good time. I have no idea why I left and went back to a Baptist Church. I met two of the Clark Sisters (Twinkie & Dorinda), Iona Locke (an amazingly awesome evangelist) Vickie Winans,

Reverend Marvin Winans, LaShaun Pace and many, many wonderful God-filled people.

Most importantly, I am thankful that I was able to receive God's forgiveness. 2 Chronicles 7:14 says if we would humble ourselves and pray and seek the face of God, and turn from our wicked ways, then will we hear from heaven, then will He forgive our sins, then will He heal our land. But there is work that we must do. I am so glad He gave me a chance to do all those things. Today I walk in total victory, total deliverance, and ain't nobody mad but the devil. God is not through with me yet.

Chapter 17
Golden Birthday Year 2002

January 31, 2002 was the year I truly desired to see. I turned 50: it was my Golden birthday. The previous year in October, I had received my Doctorate degree. I was on cloud nine. The year seemed so different. On New Year's Eve, only Ebony and I were home. Marilyn was at her home, recuperating from surgery. Mark was vacationing and Jaray, Jr. was with his wife and his new daughter. At midnight, the telephone started ringing," It was my children. "Happy New Year, Ma!" It was Jaray, Jr. I called Marilyn because she had just had surgery. We greeted and wished each other New Year's blessings. Lil Ebony and I had already prayed. Every year my children knew we would be in church, praying in the New Year, or at home, praying together. That particular year, I cooked greens, black-eyed peas, fried chicken, potato salad, and corn bread. Because not all of my children were at home, it felt strange, really empty.

This same month, I celebrated my pastoral anniversary. 2002 was a very special year. God had blessed me to serve as pastor for the previous seven Years at MG's Full Gospel, and now I was approaching my golden age. Each Sunday, we were blessed to have great speakers. I was personally blessed to have received many congratulatory awards from assembly persons, Congresswomen, a Senator, the LA Unified School District Superintendent, and the California Governor.

On the last Sunday in January, one speaker spoke on the subject, "Fear to Faith" and another minister (Mary Mary' father) related the story about his one and only son's death. He said how he had been so inspiring to other people in the time of them losing their children. He shared how painful it was losing his son and how God had helped him to heal. It was so touching. That night, January 27th, my two older children (Marilyn and Jaray, Jr.) came up for prayer and rededicated their lives to the Lord. I remember the thrill of it all and praising God. This was the greatest day of my life to see my son, daughter, and about four other young people rededicate themselves to the Lord.

On the next day, January 28, Jaray, Jr. said, "Ma, let's go for a long ride, just the two of us. I want to spend quality time with you." He dressed in his nice dark-blue suit and his black Kangol hat and off we drove, going toward San Diego. We stopped and had breakfast, looking at beautiful homes on the way. Jr. said, "I'm riding with d-doctor. We laughed, and I told him he could be a doctor, lawyer, or anything he wanted to be. We went shopping and bought his baby her first goldfish and some clothes.

Later, we stopped, ate dinner together, and he wished me a happy birthday. When we arrived home, he could not wait to take his five-month old baby her goldfish. He asked me if he could work at my childcare center doing odd jobs, so he would have money to send to his wife for his daughter, Sara. Instead of paying him, he had me send the money to Sara via certified mail. Sara's mother did not accept the mail.

February arrived with Valentine's Day. Jr. got me a card and a rose. I was so happy. This son of mine was a special kind of person. (My angel!) He could humor people and turn lemons into refreshing lemonade.

On February 2, 2002, the Gospel host of KJLH came to my church to commemorate my golden year. We had jumbo jumps, games, barbeque, potato salad, greens, yams, fried chicken, Cajun rice, chicken sausage, cake and sodas. We had so much fun and Christian fellowship together. Jr. helped cut the ribs with Momma and some of his friends came to celebrate this wonderful and great occasion. When he left, he told me how proud of me he was. It was Marilyn's birthday this month, too. We celebrated it by having dinner together.

March arrived. It was a nice, quiet month. Jr. worked at his job and helped his sister at her beauty shop, where she worked in the evenings. He would shampoo hair and clean the floor. He would then come home and go through his routine: kiss my forehead, take a shower, then go and hang out for a couple of hours. I cautioned him, and he would say that I was worrying too much. "I am alright," he would say I am covered with the Blood of Jesus." Neither my mom nor I wanted him to stay in the neighborhood anymore, even though he grew up in it, because so many shootings occurred.

When my sons were growing up, they were taught boys and men did not cry. This particular month Jr. started crying in front of us, but would not tell us what was bothering him.

Certainly one thing that bothered him deeply was that he was denied access to his baby, Sara. I reminded him to hold on because God had his back.

Easter was on the way. The two of us went shopping and got his daughter and his stepson an Easter basket. He felt happy. Easter Sunday, his wife, and lil Sara came over and ate Easter dinner with us. I was happy. We took pictures and just relaxed.

April brought beautiful sunshiny weather and flowers bloomed. My brother, Aston, was having domestic problems. I determined I would not get involved. But, I ended up going to Louisiana to support him. Jr. went too, so nothing would happen to his Ma. We stayed at my brother's house. My brother's court day arrived. He got upset, so Jr. took him outside by the Mississippi River and talked to him. When they returned to the courtroom, my brother, Aston, had a new attitude. Jr. was a peacemaker.

He went by to visit his paternal relatives. They were happy to see him. His grandmother fixed dinner for him and his aunt fixed his hair in a new style (braids).

He visited my dad. He told Jaray, Jr. to be a good boy and bought him a black suit. Jr. was very grateful.

Then we flew home first class and the flight crew was extra nice to "Mr. Charmer." They served him more than enough and gave him a bottle of wine as we exited the airplane. He was getting ready for his 24th birthday.

When we arrived home, it was Momma's birthday, April 21st. We all went out to dinner, the whole family. We all had so much fun being together. Momma is the oldest on her side of the family and it was a great celebration.

I started planning for our annual Mother's Day celebration. On May 10th, all the ladies in my family and the ladies from the neighborhood that were mothers came to my house. No men or children were allowed. We had nameplates for all the guests and enjoyed scrupulous delicious mouth watering King Crab Legs, boiled shrimp with a special dip that I make and other delicacies.

Although no men were allowed, guess who showed up? "Mr. Personality" (Jr.) He walked around the table and gave all the ladies a kiss and a promise of a $20.00 bill.

Shockingly, three days later, my sensitive, loving son was served with restraining orders from his wife and was forced to go to court.

In May, Jaray, Jr. appeared in court. I just did not want to go. This was some crazy stuff. Why was he going through so much? I gave him some encouraging words and told him I was praying for him. I gave one of my employees off and she went with him and Marilyn was already at the courthouse waiting for him to support him.

He acted proper and never lost his composure. His mother- and father-in-law witnessed how he was very respectful with excellent manners. They testified that they had never seen Jr. hit or abuse their daughter. He handled his case very well under those difficult circumstances. I was very proud of him. His heart was very heavy but he still tried to keep that lovely smile on his face.

Memorial Day Weekend, I got a call from Jaray, Jr.'s first child. He asked me to come to his Pre-K graduation. I hesitated and told him I was going to send him something nice. But, he said, "Granny, *PLEASE.*" I gave in and told him okay. Then I informed Jr. that we needed to make reservations to see his son, and my grandson, graduate. Jaray, Jr. was real happy. We packed, bought tickets, and flew to Little Rock, Arkansas.

James' mother and grandparents were very happy to see us. James jumped in his daddy's arms like he was a little baby. They had talked on the telephone, but they had not seen each other since James was 17-months-old. What a delight it was to see my son and grandson reunite and start bonding. James is my first grandson and my college surprise from when his daddy was attending Philander Smith College.

We all went to dinner that night. Jr. asked James' mother to forgive him for any hurt and pain that he had put her through. He told her he realized he had made mistakes.

The next day, we went to the graduation and videotaped and took pictures of the ceremony. It was a very hot day. James had his little face frowned up because of the sun and Jr. had an umbrella over the two of us.

That Friday night, James and his little brother Javon stayed at the hotel with Jr. and me while their mother went out on a date. He followed his daddy everywhere he went. It was like Mini Me. They both were laughing and were so happy together. The next morning we got up, ate breakfast and we went to the swimming pool. Jr. took the time to help James get rid of the fear of the water for swimming. I was thrilled to see his parenting with James in action. Javon was a little boy with personality galore. He would not let James and Jaray, Jr. be to themselves. He let them know, "I am here, too. I want to swim, too." It was hilarious. Jaray, Jr. was handling two little boys. James actually showed that he wanted his daddy to himself. He told Javon, "This is my daddy. You have your own dad-de."

Later, James' maternal grandparents came to get him. James really did not want to say good-bye to his dad. They hugged, kissed, and did a high five. When he kissed me, his maternal stepgrandmother let him say a scripture to me, "Granny, *I can do all things through Christ Jesus who strengthens me.*" Oh my God, I was so elated. I hugged him and told him to call me collect whenever he felt like it. Then we flew back to California.

The month of June arrived. I told Jaray, Jr. to go and stay with his daddy and give me a break because I was not feeling good. I had headaches and chest pains. Of course, he did not want to leave me, but did. Yet, he would come every evening to see about me before he went home.

On Thursday, June 20th, I became very ill. An ambulance rushed me to the hospital. As soon as my children found out, all of them came rushing in the emergency room.

Jaray, Jr. looked at the heart monitor and said, "You ought to stop faking; you're gonna be alright." He took my right foot and shook it. I was hospitalized seven days.

Upon discharge, Jaray Jr. wanted to stay with me, but I insisted that he stayed with his dad. All the oldest children were with him (Marilyn, Mark and now Jr.)

July 18, my mother called me and told me Marilyn's godfather had passed away, and that his funeral services were being held on July 26, 2002. On Sunday, July 21, I announced to the church that we would be having prayer meeting Tuesday night, Wednesday night, and Friday night until midnight. I had never announced prayer meetings three times a week in all of my seven years of pastoring. I often ask the Lord to order my steps and to keep me in His will. I felt this was His will and I was obedient unto it. It was sooooooooooo strange.

July 19, I had a vision, or dream. My mom called me and said a friend had called her. In this vision or dream, I replied that we were preparing to bury one of our own family members, too. It was frightening. When I was telling momma about this vision, she responded, "Girl don't say that." Though I did not know it, My God was preparing me for *"THE TERRIBLE NIGHT."*

Chapter 18
The Calling

In retrospect, I realize leaving Academy Cathedral may not have been the best choice, particularly after so many spiritual deposits had been made in my life. Yet and still, I found myself leaving there and joining the Missionary Baptist Church. The minister said something to the entire congregation that disturbed my spirit. He informed us that he was putting all members on probation that were not tithing. I thought to myself, "Didn't Jesus walk this earth to save people and heal the sick?" How would he like it if God had put him on probation for something he came short on? Although I was tithing, I still left the church. I could not understand his perfection.

After that, I started attending church services where my family owned the building. It was a Full Gospel church. I liked the services and there was a lot of teaching going on. The Pastor at the time had a history of not making his rent payments. He made statements in front of my mother and stepfather that he would remain at the location in my family's building until they put him out. But the very next Sunday when I happily arrived at the building on time for services, the Pastor came in, put a sign on the door with the church's new location, and told me to follow him there because they were moving. I could not believe what I was hearing and seeing. He had just made a contrary statement last Sunday. However, his rent was behind a couple of months. Wow!!! I looked at him and stayed right in my seat. I heard a still voice speak to me, "Be still, and know that I am God." **(Psalms 46:10)** I stayed that morning; it was just God and me. I had a little talk with Jesus, and I told him about my heart and what I was feeling. It would be just a short time after that when I would realize God was preparing me for the pulpit.

As I continued to ponder what I was feeling, I remembered that while I was at the Academy, there was a lot of healing, fasting, praying and anointing. I was around the anointing and we cried and we prayed and were joyful for one another. Unlike Pastor Smith's church, no one had a special seat to be seated in. I could feel the spirit. I was having dreams that I was floating in the air and I could just fly. I knew that God had done a new thing in me. I started being in love with Jesus. I knew I was on to something real. I knew that it was better than mmmm mmmm good. It was better than sex, drugs and alcohol. I had begun to experience a peace that surpasses all understanding. It was the goodness and graciousness of God.

God spoke to me and told me, "Daughter, I want you to be a messenger to carry my Word." I thought He meant teach Sunday School. I got another message. God said, "I want you to carry my Word." At that point I started ministering to my students and telling them who Jesus is. Again, I got the word, "Daughter I want you to carry my Word." After I had gone through the test, I ended up with a testimony. I realized that there was a call on my life that was deeper than teaching Sunday school or ushering. **I had to minister to young people.**

After the last test, Jaray, Jr. and Mark and I started canvassing the neighborhood for unsaved youth and I started having services in my garage having services until we had outgrown the garage of my home in Inglewood, California on 108th Street. After we outgrew that space, we moved into a large building on 65th Street and Normandie. This move was one that I can testify and say I know it was the Lord's doing. I never paid a day's rent nor asked for anything of the members but tithes and offering. I was obedient and I felt an inner peace. It seemed like God had exhaled his breath on me. I was happy and my children were also.

My sons, Jaray, Jr., Mark and I talked to some of their associates, classmates and friends in the neighborhood, and many of them attended. We had good church services. Some played the drums and the piano. We sang and everybody had a testimony. It didn't matter if the testimony was as simple as, "Thank you, Jesus, for allowing me to be here in the house of the Lord one more time." I taught the Word. It wasn't too long before we outgrew the garage.

My family allowed me to have services at the building that had just become vacated. This church became MG's Full Gospel Nonde-nominational Church. M and G are the initials of my late maternal Grandmother Mary. God had it in His plan. We baptized over 150 people in "God's Water," i.e. the Pacific Ocean. Not only did we baptize, but we performed weddings, funerals, did counseling, visited the sick and the shut-in and fed the hungry.

During this time, I decided to further my education. I applied and was accepted to a Ph.D. program in Pastoral Ministry in August 1999 and graduated after completing my dissertation on the subject, "Women Pastors in the Local Church." Being a woman-Pastor has been a very challenging, but rewarding job. Thus far, I have successfully celebrated thirteen wonderful pastoral anniversary services with my co-workers in Christ. There has never been a dress code for the church. I believe what Jesus said, "Come as you are." My children were all members of MG's. We baptized Lil Ebony, my youngest child. We gave to the needy. We loved. We knew each other by name, and we could sit around and be the body of Christ together. I truly miss my congregation in California. I still love each and every one of them, my evangelist and minister friends.

I live in Georgia now and have a ministry entitled "Healing Hurting Women." We have a joyous time in serving God. I am still a Pastor. I don't feel like you can lose what a marvelous gift God has given you once you get it and ask Him to order your steps. I feel that I have truly been blessed. I am a woman of faith and do believe that God will supply all of your needs according to His riches in glory. He will give you the desires of your heart if you delight yourself in Him. I am soooooo glad that I got rid of that spirit telling me I had to have a husband to be blessed and successful. I do believe that there is someone for everyone. My situation was just that I did not wait on the Lord. I have no other choice now but to believe and wait on Him. I know God has all the answers. He does not change and He knows my heart. Forget about all these judgmental people. I know where my help and my strength come from. As Marvin Sapp so beautifully sings, "I never could have made it" without the Lord, I too can attest to that. Thank God for His grace and mercy. He placed so many influential ladies in my life; most of them don't even know it: Vickie Winans, Iona Locke, Joyce Meyers, Marilyn Hickey, my grandmother (Mary), my great great aunt (Aunt Elaine - who bought my first piano) and my mother (Ebony).

I find myself counseling and ministering each and every day of my life because I know how good and how great God is.

Chapter 19
A Charge to Keep I Have

In my previous published account of my life of ill repute, all of the readers wanted to know who these men were. Well, it really doesn't matter. One must realize that in such situations, women are usually the ones branded as the whores or throwing themselves on men. But naming these men can cause one of two things to happen. They will either increase membership for the wrong reasons, or their names will soon be forgotten. You must understand that we all will have to answer to the Lord with repentance.

I'm not trying to put any one on "Front Street;" that's not the purpose of this book. I just want to bring some awareness to what could happen. I believe someone needed to be open enough to make the young innocent aware. My prayer is that I have done so tactfully.

Also, I am not trying to hurt the wives of the men involved because every one of the ministers was married. There was never a single man in any room we were ever in. I was not the only female from our congregation. As I was entering the hotels on some occasions, when I would run into the ladies from the church, for many years, I thought it was coincidental. I never thought they were coming and going out of the same room. Later on through the years some of these women were having babies that looked just like Pastor Smith. People were talking about them but it didn't even dawn on me that there could be any validity. I could have been one also that was being talked about, too. But I thank God that none of my children belong to Pastor Smith. Ironically, he had a long marriage that produced two wonderful daughters and a son that he would talk about all the time.

Just in 2007, I heard and saw one of these ministers preaching a sermon on national TV. It bothered me that he tried to degrade Kobe Bryant and his famous infidelity scandal. I thought, "How could he make such a judgment call, knowing full well that he was one of the Pastors I served up for Pastor Smith?" I sat down and said to myself, "You low life bastard. Do you remember me and others at the Airport Park Hotel when you visited Los Angeles? I don't know Kobe but how dare you point the finger? I was in my early twenties and you gave me a nice sum of money for our little fling. REMEMBER? I dare not say here in 2007.If the people only knew. There they were raving and shouting over this sermon with **YOU,** an adulterous preacher!"

This Pastor isn't the only one. But the facts surrounding the others are neither here nor there. It doesn't matter anymore. I have carried all this hurt around for as long as I can remember. I thank God that He has allowed me to forgive myself and to ask His forgiveness. I must go on with my life in a positive and godly way.

Through all my secrets, sin, struggle, stress, and surviving, I've been blessed. We all have a story to tell or skeletons in our closet. I don't mind sharing my story because it was therapeutic for me. I strongly hope I can help some young lady or ladies that have been abused in the church or keep them from being abused. I also hope this helped heal a hurting mother who might have lost her child to a violent crime. Lastly, I fervently hope that my testimony can aid hurting women who have been physically or mentally abused by their spouses.

The scripture exhorts elderly women to teach the young women. I was ashamed before, but not anymore. I am not happy over what has happened, nor am I crying about my life. I only want to help educate the ladies that get caught up in this madness. I am holding up my head up with much dignity.

As Joel Osteen says, "It's a wrong thinking pattern that keeps us imprisoned in defeat." I had been programmed to so many negative thoughts by relatives, some ministers, some teachers, and some friends. If I had listened to them, I'd believe their words which said, "I would never make it." As you can see, those were lies. My time is now. I must forget about my past.

Everything I've gone through is over. My past cannot and will not determine my future. God said that He would give me a "twofold recompense for my former shame." That means if I keep the right attitude, God will pay me back double for my trouble. God will add up all the injustices, all the hurts, and the pains that people have caused me.

After reading and seeing the spiritual seduction, I am more than convinced that after all I have gone through that I am to be grateful.

Chapter 20

Jesus Paid it All for Me

Yes, Jesus paid it all. All to Him I owe. **Sin had left a Crimson Stain**

But guess what? _**He washed it, White as Snow**_.

If Jesus has forgiven me for spiritual seduction in my life and I have forgiven myself by being strong enough to let go and let God, you can also be forgiven of your secrets, sin and stress. I am a witness that you can yet survive.

Please do not criticize nor judge me. Matthew 7: 1-2 says, "Judge not, that ye be not judged. For with what judgment ye judge, ye shall be judged; and with what measure ye mete, it shall be measured to you again."

If it's hard to understand, we all live in a glass house, we none can afford to throw a stone. Take a look into the mirror and judge the image starring back at you.

I do also believe that we have all sinned and come short of the glory of God but if you are a true believer, you will understand the concept, "We fall down but we get up."

I praise God that His darling son Jesus paid it all for me and you.

As I close these chapters in my life and as you have read, you may have identified something in this story and you would like to give your heart and soul to God and invite Him in.

Please read loud:
Dear God:

Here I am,
Just you and me.
I know you love me
More than I have loved myself.
Forgive me for all of my sins and transgressions.
I openly and willing accept you in my life
As my personal savior.
Thank you, Lord, for giving me another chance.
I accept you right now.
I know that it is your will and not mine.
I want a new start as of this minute,
And I thank you right now in the mighty name of Jesus.

Amen

If you accepted Christ and do not have a church, I invite you to call me for prayer, (678) 491-5644 or go to:
www.mgsministries.com

Book Club Study Questions

- Does the book trigger any parallels in your life that you need to be delivered from?

- Can you identify some strong holds that may have made it difficult for Stacey/Angela to get out of the lifestyle?

- What does the book bring to mind when it comes to making mature decisions?

- How do you now view your own spiritual life?

- Have you ever been naïve and made foolish choices as a result?

- Would you forgive someone if they exploited you as Pastor Smith exploited Stacey/Angela?

- Was Stacey/Angela a victim?

- Do you think Stacey/Angela was willing to stay with her husbands or was Reverend Smith a get-away for her?

- Do you think Reverend Smith was right/wrong for encouraging her to come out with him and his co-pastors and other colleagues? Why? Why not?

Aout the Author

Gloria M. Milow, PhD, is a native of New Orleans, Louisiana and is a multi-talented woman of God who operates under the gifts of teaching, counseling, and pastoring. Raised in a family of educators, she has 34 years of teaching experience, sixteen of which were spent as a counselor and psychologist. Dr. Milow is also the founder and pastor of MG's Full Gospel Church.

A learned woman, Dr. Milow's educational accomplishments include an Associate of Arts degree, Bachelor of Science in English, Sociology and Psychology, a Master of Arts with honors in Education Psychology specializing in Counseling and a Doctorate of Philosophy in Pastoral Ministry. Dr. Milow appears in "Who's Who in America," and presently serves as President for "Advocacy United," a Toastmaster's organization.

She holds three lifetime credentials in California in the following areas: Counseling, English, Psychology, and Sociology and in the state of Georgia an education leadership certificate.

The talented entrepreneur has operated many successful businesses including Classie Fashions by Marie, Milow's Nitey-Nite Child Care, Buying and Retailing Cars, Event Planning, Young Adults Ministry, and Counseling.

Dr. Milow has made guest appearances in media outlets such as WAOK 1380AM (Georgia), KJLH 102.3 Front Page (Los Angeles/Inglewood), Tom Pope Show (Washington, DC) and a host of other radio and television programs. She also appeared in a segment of The Michael Baisden Show called "Pimps in the Pulpit," and "The Grave Digger's Show" on the Angel Network. She was also one of the nominees for the Steve Harvey's Hoodie in Awards 2007 and 2008.

In spite of great personal challenges, Dr. Milow has managed to pluck victory out of life's ashes. *Spiritual Seduction* reflects some of the ashes of her life: secrets, sin, struggle, stress and surviving, and they each attest to her determination to survive. Not only has she survived; she has overcome and started "Healing Hurting Women's Seminars." She is also a motivational speaker.

Order Form

To order additional copies, fill out this form and send it along with your check or money order to:

MG's Books
3645 Marketplace Blvd
Suite 130-110
East Point, Georgia 30344

Cost per copy US $15.95 Canada $20.00 plus $2.50 P&H.

Ship _____ copies of *Spiritual Seduction* to:
Name:_____

Address:_____

City/State/Zip:_____

E-mail:_____
___ Check for signed copy

Please tell us how you found out about this book.

___ **Friend**	___ **Internet**
___ **Book Store**	___ **Radio**
___ **Newspaper**	___ **Magazine**
___ **Other** _____	

Allow two weeks for shipping.
Visit us online at:
www.mgsbooks.com or www.mgsministries.com.